Saint Patrick's People

Also by Tony Gray

FICTION

Starting from Tomorrow
The Real Professionals
Gone the Time
Interlude
The Last Laugh

NON-FICTION

The Irish Answer
The Record-Breakers (*with Leo Villa*)
Psalms and Slaughter
Buller (*with Henry Ward*)
Champions of Peace
The White Lions of Timbavati (*with Chris McBride*)
Some of My Best Friends are Animals
(*with Terry Murphy*)
Operation White Lion (*with Chris McBride*)
The Road to Success: Alfred McAlpine, 1935–85
Fleet Street Remembered
Mr Smyllie, Sir
Europeople
Ireland This Century

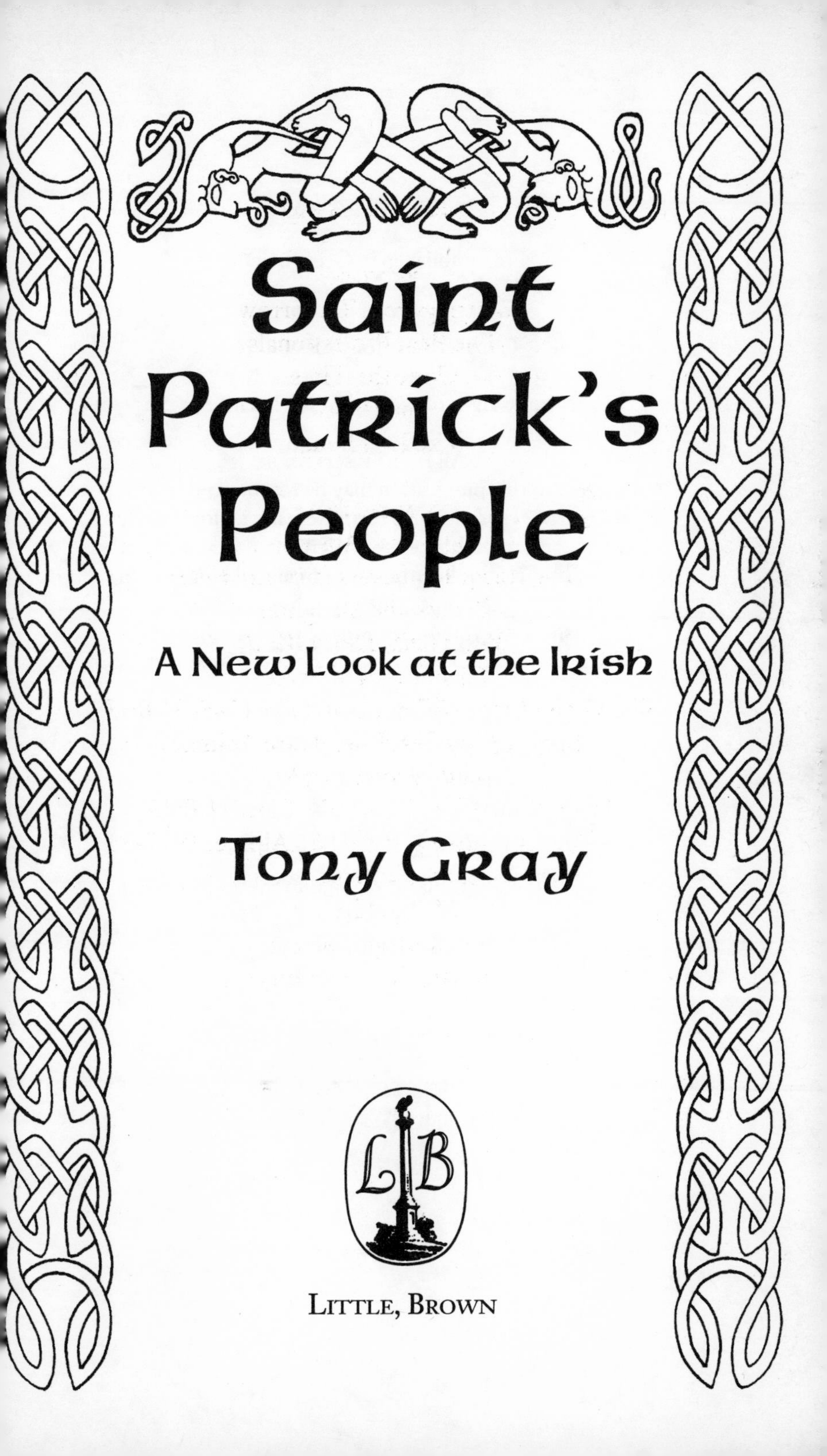

Saint Patrick's People

A New Look at the Irish

Tony Gray

Little, Brown

A *Little, Brown* Book

First published in Great Britain
by Little, Brown and Company 1996

A CIP catalogue record for this book is available
from the British Library.

ISBN 0 316 87712 3

Typeset by Solidus (Bristol) Limited
Printed and bound in
by Clays Ltd, St Ives plc

Little, Brown and Company (UK)
Brettenham House
Lancaster Place
London WC2E 7EN

For my brother, Ken,
who came up with the splendid title of this book,
and who has helped me, over the years,
in all sorts of ways.

Contents

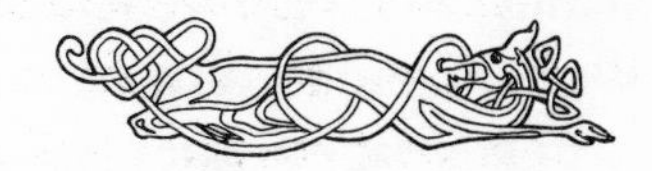

Introduction

Saint Patrick's Island: The People or the Place?

When I started to research this book I set out to try to discover who the Irish people really are, and what it is that makes them so different from everybody else, so different even from other Celts. They are quite different from the Welsh, the Bretons, the Cornish, and the Scots and yet they come from exactly the same racial stock. In the case of the Scots, from precisely the same two basic racial stocks. The first people to arrive in Ireland – they turned up during the Stone Age – were the Picts; we know very little about them but we do know that they arrived in Ireland from Scotland, and we also know that the Celts of Scotland originally went there from Ireland. The Irish Celts who settled in Scotland were called the *Scotiae* by the Romans; that's how Scotland came to get its name.

Yet although there are superficial similarities – a certain common whimsy in their folklore and poetry, a shared fondness for a drop of the hard stuff every now and then – the Scots and the Irish are fundamentally poles apart.

The Scots are characterised as tidy, thrifty, canny,

close, industrious, provident, and almost embarrassingly honest.

The Irish are characterised as untidy, profligate, happy-go-lucky, generous both of their time and their worldly goods, almost to a fault; they spend money like drunken sailors, they will always lie to you if they feel that a lie will please you better than the truth, they will never do anything today that can be put off until tomorrow or next year, and they are as laid back as any of the inhabitants of California or the Mediterranean littoral, despite their wet and chilly climate.

Causes which might have contributed something to the strangeness of the Irish – and I don't use that word in any pejorative sense – are many and varied. Alone of almost all our European neighbours, apart from the Scandinavian countries, Ireland was never invaded and colonised by the Romans. The Irish were never subjected to the discipline of straight Roman roads and rigid Roman laws; nor did they ever have the opportunity of sampling, even at second hand, such decadent delights as central heating and Roman baths.

Alone of almost all our European neighbours, again with the exception of the Scandinavian countries, Ireland was not over-run after the Fall of the Roman Empire by any of the barbarian hordes who came from somewhere east of the Danube; in fact, from the fall of Rome in the fifth century until the first Viking invasions at the beginning of the eleventh, Ireland enjoyed a period of peace and prosperity unparalleled elsewhere on mainland Europe.

The very fact that Saint Patrick and his Breton assistants, who converted the Irish to Christianity and taught them how to read and write both in their own language and in Latin, happened to be Celts themselves, meant that the old Celtic pagan gods were never totally banished, but were integrated into a form of Christianity which was in itself unique in Europe.

It had to be. Because elsewhere in Europe, the diocesan organisation of the Church was based on the well-established local government framework of existing towns and cities; and there were no towns and cities in Ireland. As a result, and as a result of the fact that the island of Britain – intervening between Ireland and mainland Europe – had been conquered by assorted Germanic tribes of Angles, Saxons and Jutes, there was not much communication between Ireland and Rome. Consequently, the Irish Church developed on completely independent lines; the monastic settlements were the principal centres of civilisation and culture in Ireland, and the regular clergy, by their very nature, tended to run things their own way, without any reference to Rome.

And although Irish missionaries carried their own version of the Christian message, and all the learning that went with it, all over the continent and indeed far further afield, Ireland was the only country in Christendom that contributed nothing, in terms of men, *matérial*, ships or funds, towards any of the crusades against the infidel.

Also, unlike the Spanish, the Portuguese and the Greeks, who share Ireland's position as among the least privileged members of the European Community in terms of material wealth, Ireland never had a great overseas empire. Almost alone among the European states, in fact, Ireland has experienced colonialism only at the receiving end: as a colony of the Anglo-Normans, who became the British.

But, in the last analysis, it seems unlikely that any of

these factors really proved decisive. For the Irish, the decisive factor, the thing that made them different from all the other nations of Europe, was the nature of the land itself: the island of Ireland. The same thing had applied to the ancient Greeks. They had come from all over the place – some of the earliest inhabitants of the Greek mainland were Celts – but it was the land, the Greek landscape that fused them, not exactly into a nation, but into a culture and focused their instincts and energies and made them unique as a race.

The argument over whether it is the people who make the place, or the place which makes the people, has been going on since men first learned to talk and exchange opinions. When you are dealing with an enormous, diverse, sprawling, amorphous landscape like central Europe, the people who happen to find themselves inhabiting any particular part of that place can make of it what they will; the Teutons and Saxons could easily turn their area into Germany, the Flemish and the Walloons could Belgianise their bit, the Dutch could add canals and tulips and windmills and personalise their corner.

But you couldn't – at any rate until fairly recently, with the arrival of the marvels of twentieth-century technology, which may well prove as disastrous as they have been useful – do anything with a land as fiercely resistant to human interference as the island of Ireland, or the mainland and isles of Greece, except try to learn to live with the place, in it, of it, from it; in the case of Greece and Ireland, certainly, it was the uniqueness of the place that made the people unique.

That may be why the descendants of the Lowland Scottish farmers (who were Irish anyway, though they had picked up some different ideas during the centuries they lived on the mainland) and those of the stout English yeomen who were brought in to re-populate and settle the province of Ulster after the collapse of the last great Irish Catholic and Celtic stand against Elizabethan England, nearly four hundred years ago, are every bit as Irish as the rest of the people in the country; they don't realise it, and they wouldn't admit it for a moment, but as soon as they are abroad anywhere, they are instantly recognised as Irish, and as nothing else. The landscape was probably too strong for them; they couldn't resist its pressures.

I'll go into all these questions in more detail in the following pages. At this stage, it's enough to say that I believe that it was Ireland which made the Irish, and not the other way around; and that Saint Patrick's people owe their very distinctive identity far more to the magical influence of that remote little, wet little, beautiful little island out in the Atlantic, on the far fringe of Europe, than they do to anything else . . .

 1 

Undiscovered and Uninhabited

Geology and Prehistory

Until fairly recently, in geological or even in archaeological terms (until, say, around six thousand years ago), the island now known as Ireland remained undiscovered and uninhabited, still in the firm grip of the ice floes. Before the last Ice Age, which ended about 10,000 years ago, animals such as the mammoth, the hyena and the reindeer roamed the area, and there were apples, hazel nuts and other fruits of the forest freely available. But there is no evidence that any of the early Stone Age hunters or gatherers ever crossed the sea to Ireland, or even walked there, as they so easily could have done.

There had been men wandering all over Europe for nearly 70,000 years, and Ireland didn't become an island until about 50,000 years ago, so during the 20,000 years or so before that, to get there would have meant only a relatively short stroll up from the Iberian peninsula. Relatively short, that is, for people who had hoofed it all the way up from central Africa, or possibly across from China, via the fertile crescent. No evidence of human habitation, or even human presence, on that tiny fragment of the earth's surface that eventually became Ireland, has been dated any earlier than about 6,000 years ago, or approximately 4,000 BC.

Ireland was then part of a continent that stretched all the way up from the peninsula that is now Spain and Portugal, and right across to the Middle East and on through Russia, India and China to the far eastern shores of the North Pacific. Towards Britain, however, a deep fissure is widely believed to have existed in the area of today's Irish Sea, which means that Ireland, so far from being an appendix of what is now Britain, was in those days part of mainland Europe, though joined to a different part of it; England was then still connected to France and the Low Countries. Or possibly Ireland was part of a surviving section of a different continent altogether, which later became detached or covered by the ocean.

The flora of Ireland point to this. According to Charles Garnier's *A Popular History of Ireland* (Cork: Mercier Press, 1961), 'Ireland's plants include several species foreign to Britain, but native to the American coastline of the same latitude, notably the blue-eyed Iris.' On the other hand, he argues, the mistletoe and narcissus, common enough in Britain, are not native Irish plants.

So, Ireland could once have been a part of the North American continent, or it could be, as Garnier suggests, that the peculiar nature of Ireland's geology, as well as of its flora and fauna, seem to support the theory of a lost continent, possibly Atlantis, first mentioned by Plato in his *Dialogues*, written somewhere around 355 BC. Plato postulated the existence of an island continent somewhere out in the ocean, away beyond the Pillars of Hercules (Gibraltar) destroyed by a great flood, or submerged in a tidal wave after a cataclysmic earth tremor, in one night and one day about 9,000 years earlier. Many people still believe that Atlantis existed and regard it as the putative site of the biblical Garden of Eden and the Celtic *Tir na nOg**, the land of everlasting youth, also known as Hy Brasil, the Island of the Blessed, for which Saint Brendan the Navigator set sail, from Brandon Creek, County Kerry and stumbled across the American continent, nine centuries before Columbus.

However, whether Atlantis ever existed or not, the geology and vegetation of Ireland would seem to indicate that Ireland is not only an entirely separate and different country from its next-door neighbour, the far from United Kingdom and former headquarters of the British Empire, but also a far older one. England, the land of the Angles – or Pritain, as the Welsh Celts called it, with a 'P' and not a 'B', long before the arrival of the Romans and five or six centuries before the arrival of the Anglo-Saxons – did not break away from the European continent and become an island until about 10,000 years ago, when the sea flooded the flatlands between the estuaries of the Rhine and the Seine to become the English Channel and the North Sea.

In my first geography lesson, I was informed that Ireland was an island shaped like a saucer.

This statement did not in any way enhance my opinion

*Pronounced, roughly, Tear-nan-Ogue. For a general note on Irish pronunciation, see Appendix.

of the teacher because, whether you looked at the map behind her or out of the window at the genuine article, it was so patently at variance with all the facts. On the map, Ireland appears to be shaped rather like a teddy bear, facing westwards towards the United States. And the genuine article, I realised even as early as that, is one of the most heart-breakingly beautiful collection of hills, valleys, mountains and lakes in the entire world.

I later learned that what the teacher probably meant was that the hills and mountains in Ireland are roughly situated around the coastline, and that the centre of the country is a plain. But even that is true only to a limited extent because there are no mountains whatever along the east coast between Howth Head and Carlingford Lough, and very few between the Wicklow Mountains and Waterford. If this proves anything, it proves that it is dangerous to over-simplify any subject, even a relatively simple one like geography, though to a writer brought up in daily newspapers, the temptation to over-simplify remains irresistible.

So, Ireland is an island in the path of the Gulf Stream, roughly about the same size as Austria or the state of Alabama. It is saucer-shaped to the extent that most of its mountains and hills are situated around the deeply indented coastline, and the centre is a great plain, part peat-bog, part limestone pasture-land. It has been an island for some 450,000 years, and it remained uninhabited for 64,000 years after primitive man (and woman, too, let's not get involved in any debates about political correctness at this early stage) first graced the continent of Europe with their presence.

The first inhabitants of the island came over from what is now Scotland and settled in the north-eastern part of the country around 6,000 BC. They were a Stone Age people, probably Picts, whoever they may have been, and they were shortly followed by another, later Stone Age people who had come from the Near East via Iberia and Brittany and had learned how to herd domestic animals and cultivate crops. These were a dark-skinned race, and they arrived around 5,000 BC. They were followed by waves of Bronze Age men. Between them, they all left plentiful samples of their pottery, arms and implements as well as fragments of their burial places. The Stone Age men raised great monuments to their dead in the material which gave them their title; their successors also worked copper, gold and bronze, as well as continuing to make monuments with stones.

But armed only with their bronze weapons, they were no match for the iron swords and the wheeled chariots of the Celts. The word Celt comes from the Greek *keltoi*, and the Celts were widely believed to have been a tall, fair-haired race of people who came to western Europe from somewhere around the source of the Danube. They started to arrive in Ireland about 1,200 BC, both from Iberia and mainland Europe and from Britain, where they had already established fairly extensive colonies in England, Wales and Scotland. The woad-bedaubed ancient Britons who lined the cliffs of Dover when Caesar's longboats first crossed the English Channel and crunched ashore on the shingles near Deal, Kent, in 55 BC were Celts. They were perhaps, in a sense, the originators of the idea that the basic unit, so to speak, might well be the British Isles as a whole, rather than the island of Ireland. It's a point I'll take up later. Plato, in his *Laws*, described the Celts as a race of people inclined to drunkenness and much given to fighting, a definition which many people would claim is not inappropriate to their latter-day Irish descendants.

Ireland got its ancient name Erin from Eire or Eiru, one of the ancient pre-Celtic queens; in Anglo-Saxon, the island later became Eirland, or Ireland. The Celts took over the existing political divisions of the country and adapted the sacred places and practices of their predecessors, just as the Christians were to do when they arrived in Ireland. And they continued to contribute to what eventually became the largest collection of extraordinary stone structures, secular and religious, to be found within such a compact compass, anywhere in the world: a total of over 40,000 dolmens, tumuli, barrows, passage-graves, cairns, ring forts and standing stones, some with inscriptions in Ogham (see page 17), spanning over 5,000 years of human history and pre-history.

Those early inhabitants of Ireland, up to and including the Goidelic (in old Irish) or Gaelic Irish Celts, so called after the dialect they spoke, did not leave any really riveting architecture behind them, but there is a kind of mute magic about some of the Irish cromlechs, dolmens and forts which makes them curiously rewarding, if not compelling, viewing. Also there is the ever-intriguing puzzle of how they managed to manhandle such enormous lumps of rock into place without any mechanical assistance: the 'roof' of one cromlech in the demesne of Howth Castle near Dublin, by no means the biggest in Ireland, is estimated to weigh about seventy tons. The thought of a great army of Stone Age men humping rocks as big as double-decker buses halfway up a mountain-side merely to mark the site of somebody's grave has a defiant determination about it that demands admiration.

The one really impressive Irish fort, Dun Aengus,

perched along the skyline on the edge of a 300-foot cliff on Inishmore, one of the Aran Islands in Galway Bay, is an enigma. Nobody knows how old it is, or who built it, or why it should have been built there in the first place. Who was it intended to defend, and from whom?

Accepted archaeological thinking dates all ring forts within the two centuries immediately before and after the birth of Christ, which might suggest that Dun Aengus was built not by Stone Age men, but by one of the earlier waves of Celts.

But this wouldn't explain why the three concentric walls of dry-stone masonry are semi-circular, or why the defences on the Atlantic side are augmented by a Maginot Line of bristling stone stakes, jutting out of the earth at menacing angles and formidable enough to halt a regiment of tanks. Another theory is that the semi-circular Dun Aengus fastness was initially a standard circular ring fort, and that one half of it has simply fallen into the sea as the cliff was eroded away.

Or there is yet a third possibility. It could be, as some historians have suggested, that the fort was built much earlier and as a defence against aggressors, not from the east, but from the west, and that the attack which the inhabitants of the island were so obviously expecting was one from the armies of Atlantis, and that the geological disturbance which separated the Aran Islands from the Irish mainland also drowned that lost continent, while at the same time causing the Inishmore cliff-top to collapse and, in the process, bisect the fort.

At Brugh-na-Boinne (the palace or fort of the Boyne, today's New Grange), the ancient Irish were burning and burying their dead with pomp and circumstance long before King Nebuchadnezzar built the Hanging Gardens of Babylon; before the birth of Tutankhamun, the boy king of Ancient Egypt; before King Solomon built his great temple in Jerusalem; even before the Minoan civilisation reached its zenith at Knossos on the island of Crete, and was suddenly wiped out of existence by another unknown cosmic disaster.

There had been Celts arriving in Ireland from the Iberian Peninsula and from all over mainland Europe for about a thousand years before the arrival of the last wave of Celts who came mainly from Britain. Nobody knows for sure what prompted the British Celts to leave the fertile Thames Valley some time around 300 BC and face the hazards of a difficult voyage across the Irish Sea to what must have appeared a very hostile island in the dark and dangerous Atlantic Ocean; one theory is that it was a lust for gold. The British Celts knew well that there must be gold in Ireland from the artefacts of the Bronze Age artisans which had reached Britain via Iberia.

Ireland's various waves of Celtic invaders, who came from all over Europe, had only one thing in common: their Celtic language, which was the common means of communication for all of Europe north of the Latin-speaking Mediterranean littoral in the last of the centuries before the birth of Christ. The Celts couldn't read or write – though they made marks in Ogham, a system of notches on the edge of standing stones to indicate something or other – but they were far from illiterate, in its sense as uncultured. Their tradition was purely an oral one but the language disappeared – except in Ireland, Scotland, Wales, and parts of Brittany – when Julius Caesar conquered Gaul, as France was then called, and then in turn the island the Romans called Britannia.

And when the Romans in their wisdom decided not to

venture the other sixty odd miles across the Irish Sea from Britain to Ireland and impose upon the Celtic Irish tribes all the disciplines inseparable from their straight Roman roads and their strict Roman laws, they were setting the scene, though they couldn't possibly have known it, for almost eight centuries of strife that has only recently started to show some faint signs of ending.

2

Giants They Were

The Celtic Myths and Legends

'An evil eye had Balor the Fomorian. The eye was never opened save on the battle-field. Four men used to lift up the eye with a polished handle which passed through its lid. If any army looked at that eye, though they were many thousands in number, they could not resist a few warriors . . .'

This is an extract from an early Christian transcription from Celtic mythology, quoted by Sean O Faolain in *The Irish*, published in 1947. Eight years earlier, Flann O'Brien had satirised this ancient, insidious Irish tendency to exaggerate in a fake 'literal' translation from the Gaelic in his first novel *At Swim-Two-Birds*: 'Each thigh to him was to the thickness of a horse's belly, narrowing to a green-veined calf the thickness of a foal. Three fifties of fosterlings could engage with handball against the wideness of his backside, which was wide enough to halt the march of warriors through a mountain pass.'

And T. W. Rolleston, that German-educated authority on Celtic myths and legends, who was Secretary of the

Irish Literary Society in London about a century ago, recounts how, when the hero Cuchulain was dying, a satirist demanded his spear. It was a point of honour with the ancient Irish never to refuse a request from a bard, and Cuchulain replied: 'Have it, then!' and hurled it with such force that it went clean through the satirist and carried on, straight through nine other men who happened to be standing behind him, killing them all. With a mythology like that to encourage them in their fantasies, it is no wonder that the Irish have often proved a baffling and unrealistic people with whom to do business.

Giants, they were, those heroes of the old Irish folk tales. Exaggeration on this lunatic scale only makes sense when you realise that none of these myths and legends was ever written down until after the coming of Christianity and, with it, literacy. Before that they had been passed on from generation to generation, told and re-told, revised and expanded, embellished and embroidered, by generations of professional story-tellers, the traditional Irish *seanchai*.

It is not difficult to imagine the scene. The ring of breathless, expectant listeners, hanging on to the story-teller's every word, his face lit fitfully by the flickering flame from the turf fire. The tense, gesticulating figure of the story-teller himself, carried away by his own eloquence, by the fierce pride he takes in the past glories of his race, to which only he and his fellow story-tellers hold the key, as well as by the warm glow which suffuses his whole interior as he refuels the furnace, drinking great draughts of *uisge beatha*, or *eau de vie*, the water of life, as whiskey was called when it was first distilled in Ireland, and as, indeed, brandy was called when it was first produced in France.

Listen: 'Gartnan had his whole island gilded with red gold. On the arable land he had seven plough-teams. He had seven herds with seven score cows in each herd. He had fifty nets for deer, and out from the island were fifty nets for fishing. The fifty fish-nets had ropes from them over the windows of the kitchen. There was a bell on the end of each rope, on the rail, in front of the stewart. Four men used to throw the first-run salmon up to him. He himself in the meantime drank mead upon his couch.'

This is not, though it sounds like it, a transcription of a recording of a tale told by a modern *seanchai*. Traditional story-tellers existed all over Ireland until fairly recently, and there are probably a few of them left in isolated villages, though the Irish language started to disappear as a living language about a century ago and most people in Ireland spend their evenings glued to the telly these days. But the extract above comes from a legend in a manuscript quoted by Kuno Meyer, the German expert on Celtic philosophy who founded the School of Irish Learning in Dublin in 1903. It was reprinted in a paper on Irish mythology by Robert Jerome Smith in *Irish History and Culture* (Kansas University Press, 1979). It carries the unmistakable marks of the self-indulgent, alliterative, outrageous exaggeration that was part and parcel of the old oral Irish tradition.

The *seanchai* told their tales around the fire during the winter months. Starting in *Samhain* (November), some of their recitals lasted for hours on end and they had hundreds of sagas and stories in their repertoires.

Most of the narratives concerned the doings – love stories, reports of cattle raids, accounts of great battles – of the various waves of Celtic and other tribes who invaded Ireland from around 1,200 BC. From these stories it is possible to build up some sort of picture of what life was like in prehistoric Ireland, at any rate so far as the captains and the kings are concerned, as well as that of their minders – the *Fianna* of Munster and Leinster and the Red Branch Knights of Ulster, among others. They don't tell us much about the everyday life of the peasants, whose lot it was then, as it was in Dan O'Connell's day and still is, in his own phrase, to break stones, 'matter a damn who happens to be in charge of the country'.

It is probably significant that the heroes of the two great cycles of Irish mythology appear to have come from two quite different social structures. Cuchulain seems to represent a society that lived by herding cattle and cultivating crops, and clearly came from the ruling classes. Fionn MacCumhail (more commonly known as Finn McCool) and his followers, on the other hand, seem to have been a subject people who hunted for their food. And while the Ulster sagas take the form of historical records, or at least appear to be partly based on historical events, the Fenian tales appear to have come down to us mainly in the form of ballads.

The early Celts were largely nomadic. They didn't build towns or cities, though their kings and chieftains lived in mud and wattle palaces built on earthenwork foundations, such as those at Tara, Ireland's Camelot, headquarters of Ireland's Celtic High Kings. Today they are no more than a series of shallow banks and depressions that can only be properly viewed from the air, though the place has the same sort of desolate serenity which marks so many sites of vanished splendour; I am thinking of places like Delphi in Greece, and Ampurias in Catalonia, and Tarxien on the island of Malta.

Later arrivals lived in *tuatha* or townlands, roughly

equivalent to the French *communes*, and they were nomadic only to the extent that they followed the seasonal movement of their herds to and from the hill pastures, *transhumance* as the French still call it.

The High King at Tara, whose supremacy was challenged every bit as often as it was acknowledged, ruled various combinations of the other four ancient kingdoms of Ireland: Ulster, Munster, Leinster and Connaught, as well as County Meath, at one time a province in its own right, and County Kerry, still known to its inhabitants as the Kingdom of Kerry. All the kings surrounded themselves with courtiers, among whom the priests, poets, bards and story-tellers enjoyed highly privileged positions. The social structure was hierarchical, and the social unit was the extended family. The country was extremely rich in flora and fauna and, since it was very sparsely populated, the living was easy.

The better-off dwelt in wooden buildings, thatched with turf or reeds; the less prosperous in *clochan*, primitive, communal, oval-shaped beehive-like dwellings which were partly subterranean. Earlier still, their ancestors had lived in *crannogs*, dwellings built on artificial lake-islands, raised above the surface of the water on wooden piles, and accessible only via submerged, zig-zag causeways that were highly treacherous to folks unacquainted with the general layout. From archaeological reconstructions, they appear to have closely resembled the rondavals that are still being built by many African tribes.

Most of the arable land was communal, and belonged to the tribe which occupied it; such private property as existed was owned by the men, and descent was patrilineal. Women came into property only through marriage, though the women of the Irish sagas are by no means the shrinking violets of the King Arthur legends, wanly waiting for their knights in armour to return from battle. They are headstrong, sensual, feisty females, who – in a phrase delightedly dredged from the ancient manuscripts by several scholars – 'did not hesitate to offer their willing thighs' in order to achieve their aims. They were also warriors, and fought in battles on more or less equal terms with their menfolk.

Cattle were then, as they are now, Ireland's principal product, apart from people. One of the most famous of the legends, the *Tain Bo Cuailgne* (*The Cattle Raid of Cooley*), concerns an attempt by Queen Maebh (Maeve in English) of Connacht to add Don Cuailge, the finest bull in Ireland, to her herd. The Brown Bull of Cooley was said to be a remarkable beast with a back broad enough for fifty children to play hurling upon it. Maeve, the warrior queen, may well have come from an earlier race of people, many of whom survived in Connacht and who were matriarchal in their social structure, with the women heading the families and ruling the tribes. However, if the *Tain* could be said to have any central theme, it is the folly of over-valuing the desires and whims of a woman, however powerful or headstrong she may be. As Fergus, the exiled former King of Ulster dryly remarks, in one of the chronicles at the very end of the saga: 'It is the usual thing for a herd led by a mare to find itself strayed and destroyed.'

Ireland at this period was thickly forested. There were no ports or towns and few roads, though the remains of what appear to be a couple of Iron Age roads across the bogs of the central plain have recently been located. Farming and herding were the basic activities. The people used no coins; everything seems to have been valued in terms of herds of cattle. Indeed, as comparatively recently as a century and a half ago, the poet James Clarence Managan was addressing an Irish lady as 'O, Woman of Three Cows!'

The religion of the ancient Celts was Druidic. The Druid priests were known as *filidh* – the word itself means poet or professor in Gaelic, as the Irish version of the Celtic language came to be called – and the Druid priests must have had prodigious memories because their key function was to preserve, in the absence of any written records, the details of the lineage of all the kings, chieftains and principal families, along with a record of all their offspring and other historical and legal records of all sorts. They also presided over community rites, which probably included an element of animal and possibly human sacrifice, though the Irish Celts seem to have been far less bloodthirsty in this respect than their Gaulish cousins.

The Druid priests also predicted the future and acted as medicine-men, curing by natural (mainly herbal) means, as well as with complicated supernatural procedures. The people were polytheistic, in the sense that they believed in natural spirits which had to be placated, and their deities included rivers as well as holy wells, standing stones, certain trees and groves, and some animals and birds which were widely revered, if not actually worshipped.

The chief god of the Irish Celts was Dagda Mor (the great Dagda), also known as an Oll-athair (the All-father), who was so immense that he ate his porridge from a hole in the ground the size of an open-cast mine, with a spoon big enough for a man and a woman to cohabit therein comfortably. His appetite for sex was as vast as his appetite for food, and lusty sexual adventures are a recurring element in Celtic mythology.

Among their other gods were Lugh, the god of light (his counterpart in Ancient Gaul had already given his name to Lugdunum, as the Romans called Lyons in France, and he is remembered in Irish Gaelic in Lughnasa, the word for the month of August); Manannan, the ancient Irish sea-god, recalled in the name of the island in the Irish Sea, the Isle of Man; and Brigit or Brigid (who was also the Saint Brigid of the Christian faith as well as the Celtic goddess Brigantia, the great guardian of the Brigantes, the North British Celts). She was one of three sisters of the same name born to Dagda – by a mother seemingly unknown, or at least unspecified – in what today is County Kildare. Brigit came to be regarded as the founder of the Irish bloodstock industry in that she was invited to claim for herself all the land that she could cover with her cloak and, in answer, she spread it out over County Kildare, the heart and centre of the Irish horse-breeding business.

Other leading deities included Angus Og, or young Angus, the son of the Dagda by Boanna (the river Boyne), and widely regarded as the Irish god of love, whose palace was at New Grange; and Ogma, the champion of the gods, who was in charge of martial matters and was credited with having invented Ogham, that Celtic form of communication using notches cut into the edge of stones. The significance of the notches has long since largely been lost, though the letters of the Ogham alphabet have been deciphered by language experts, to their own satisfaction at any rate.

The spellings of the gods' names are, of course,

entirely arbitrary and represent attempts made by latter-day Christian scribes to reproduce the sounds they heard in the stories recounted to them by the *seanchai*.

If the Druid priests had any theories as to how the world came into existence in the first place, they don't seem to have passed them on to the bards or story-tellers. Alone among all the races of humankind, the Irish Celts possess no creation myth which purports to explain the origin of the earth. Irish accounts of the beginning of things all start with the arrival of various waves of invaders in Ireland. It could be, of course, that since all the early manuscripts date from after the coming of Christianity, and were first written down by the Christian monks, any non-Christian concepts of the creation which featured in the old myths and legends were carefully edited out and replaced by the biblical versions of the creation which appear as a prefix to many of the old manuscripts.

The old Irish manuscripts list a succession of colonies or races of people said to have invaded Ireland in prehistoric times. The first of these were the Partholanians (from Greece). Led by Partholan, they arrived in Ireland three hundred years after the Great Flood, generally assumed by traditional biblical scholars as having taken place fairly soon after the fall of Babylon, which used to be widely believed to have occurred around 600 BC. Three hundred years later, the Partholonians were all carried off by a great plague. However, since the tale exists, someone must have survived to tell it, and from the Book of the Dun Cow, written down around 1,100 AD, it appears that the survivor was Tuan, the son of a brother of Partholan's.

Tuan is said to have lived alone on the island of Ireland

for twenty-two years after the plague had killed off all the other inhabitants, until Nemed, 'the son of his father's brother', as the old manuscripts quaintly phrase it, set sail with a fleet of thirty-two barques, with thirty Nemedians in each barque, also apparently from Greece, though it could be that those early Christian scribes didn't know very much about other areas in the world from which the invaders might conceivably have arrived. On the other hand, it is equally possible that the notion that they originated in Greece could have come from the final wave of Celts themselves, who arrived in Ireland at roughly the time when Greek civilisation was at its height.

Only Nemed himself, plus four men and four women, seem to have survived the journey. They landed in Ireland, settled down, prospered and multiplied until there were precisely 8,060 of them, when they in turn just as mysteriously disappeared.

In the Celtic legends, Tuan lives on through all those centuries, in the form first of a stag and then of a wild boar. He continues to tell the tale, recalling how next the Firbolgs arrived, and survived into historic times, as did their immediate successors, the Fomorians, and the Thuatha de Danaan (the people of the goddess Dana) 'from whom all the men of learning are sprung', as the Book of the Dun Cow put it. Finally, there were the Milesians, from whom all the principal Celtic Irish families like to think they can trace their descent.

It has been suggested that the Fomorians, sometimes described as half-human monsters, represented the forces of darkness, as against the forces of light. Another interpretation of the Celtic myths is that the Tuatha de Danaan represented the priest and warrior caste, and the Fomorians the farmers and tillers of the soil, though the

Fomorians are also described in some of the legends as sea-pirates. The name of the Irish goddess Dana, or Danu (among the Welsh Celts, Don) is probably an echo of the names of the rivers Don and Danube, the area from which the Celts initially set out for western Europe, carrying their myths and legends with them.

The Celtic legends eventually encompass the coming of Christianity in the fifth century AD, as well as backwards to embrace the arrival in Ireland of many of the pre-Celtic inhabitants, among them those Firbolgs (the word means bag-men). They had lived at one period in captivity in Greece, where they had been obliged to transport earth – in leather bags, hence their name – from the fertile valleys up to the barren hilltops, so that the latter could be cultivated. Eventually they escaped from slavery, converted their leather bags into curraghs or coracles, and set sail for Iberia, from whence they travelled to Ireland. The Firbolgs were defeated in the first Battle of Magh Tuiredh (Moytura, near today's Cong, in County Mayo) by the Tuatha de Danaan, and banished to Connemara. The Fomorians subsequently invaded Ireland and held the people of Dana in servitude for many years.

The Danaan god-warrior Lugh (he was master of all the crafts as well as the god of light) summoned the fighting men of the still undefeated Danaans in Ulster to join him in a final effort to rid Ireland forever of the Fomorians, and during the second Battle of Moytura, came face to face with his own grandfather, the Fomorian Balar or Balor of the Evil Eye, whom we encountered at the beginning of this chapter. By this time Balor was so old and so frail that he had not sufficient strength to open his Evil Eye, which had lost none of its destructive properties in the meantime. When the four Fomorians raised Balor's eye-lid by its polished handle, to focus its deadly glare on the people of Dana, Lugh drove the eye back through Balor's head with a sling-stone, so that it faced to the rear and wrought destruction instead upon his own Fomorian troops, who were beaten back into the sea and were finally defeated. Ireland was once again free, and under the rule of the people of Dana.

The victorious warrior-god Lugh becomes, with the willing connivance of a young Milesian maiden Dechtera, the father of Cuchulain, the great folk-hero and warrior of the Irish Celts in the final phase of prehistoric Ireland, which is, so to speak, where we came in.

Apart, that is, from the Milesians. According to the legends, as transcribed by the early Christian monks, the Milesians were the last wave of Celtic invaders, and they were humans, not gods. They were so called after Milesius or Miledh, a mythical king of Spain, and they conquered the Tuatha de Danaan and reigned in Ireland until the coming of Christianity and the arrival, in the myths and legends of Ireland, of genuine historical events.

T. W. Rolleston, one of the first scholars to examine the Celtic myths in a scientific way, suggests that if the Tuatha de Danaan represent the forces of light and the inherent Celtic reverence for science, poetry and artistic skills, and their victory over the Firbolgs represents the victory of the intellect over darkness, dullness and ignorance (light, sharp, piercing spears overcoming heavy, blunt swords, the Iron Age conquering the Bronze Age and the Stone Age, perhaps), and the Fomorians represent the forces of tyranny, greed and cruelty, it is puzzling to find the Tuatha de Danaan in turn defeated by the

Milesians and dispossessed of their hard-won inheritance, the beautiful island of Ireland.

'What is the meaning,' he asks, in *Myths and Legends of the Celtic Races* (London: Harrap, 1911), 'of this shrinking of their powers which at once took place when the Milesians came on the scene? The Milesians were not on the side of the powers of darkness ... Was the Kingdom of Light, then, divided against itself? Or if not, to what conception in the Irish mind are we to trace the myth of the Milesian invasion and victory?'

The only answer Rolleston could find to this puzzling question was to suppose that the Milesian myth originated at a much later date than all the others, and was, in all its main features, the product of Christian influences. The earlier legends leave the beautiful, talented, cultured People of Dana in full and final possession of the country, but some at least of them were pagan divinities, and as such would never have been accepted as the true ancestors of the devout Christian Irish by the monks who wrote the legends down. Somehow or another, they had to be eliminated, and a race of less awkward antecedents substituted for them.

'So the Milesians were fetched from Spain,' he concludes, 'and endowed with the main characteristics, only more humanised, of the people of Dana, [though] the latter, in contradistinction to the usual attitude of early Christianity, are treated very tenderly in the story of their overthrow ... They are no longer gods, but they are more than human, and frequent instances occur in which they are shown as coming forth from their fairy world, being embraced in the Christian fold and entering into heavenly bliss.'

Which was, of course, the ultimate fate of the Children

of Lir, who were eventually captured in Christian times, after nine hundred years of wandering, in the form of eternally young swan-children, all over Ireland. When they finally reverted to human form, it was to reveal not the radiant, everlasting beauty of young Danaan divinities, but four withered, snowy-haired old human crones, who were hastily and mercifully baptised into the new faith before they died.

Something of the same fate awaited Eithne, handmaiden to the daughter of Mannanan Mac Lir, the Celtic sea-god. Eithne had embraced Christianity but was still constantly visited by the spirits of her Danaan kinfolk. During one of these visitations she fell to the floor in a swoon, became gravely ill, and died in the arms of Saint Patrick, who administered the last rites and saw her safely on her way to the Christian Heaven.

After their defeat, the People of Dana did not withdraw, as all the other conquered armies did, nor did they flee the country. Instead, using their magic arts, they cast over themselves the veil of invisibility, which they could shrug off whenever it suited them. Henceforward there were two Irelands, one natural and one supernatural. The Danaans lived on in the Otherworld as the People of the Sidhe (the Fairy People), still inhabiting, some people believed, their former palaces which continued to exist in all their splendour in the Otherworld, though ordinary people could see only the green mounds and ramparts and broken walls and other shattered relics of ruined fortresses and deserted dolmens. The parallel here with the Dream Time of the aboriginal Australians and the extraordinary empathy with their landscape of the native Indians of North America is very striking.

Others legends suggested that, after their defeat, the

Danaans departed to the sea-god's country, Tir na nOg, the Land of Youth, that Otherworld island out in the Atlantic somewhere, from which they would return from time to time to mix and mingle with mortal men in love and war.

And although the term the 'wee folk', or the little people, is still used whimsically in Ireland to describe fairies, those original fairies, the People of the Sidhe, whenever they cast aside their cloak of invisibility, were indistinguishable from humans. Indeed in parts of Ireland until not very long ago, many people believed in fairies who were frequently mistaken for ordinary people – ghosts in other words, though unlike ghosts elsewhere, there was nothing scary about them.

There is another theory about where the fairy folk that were the Celtic Tuatha de Danaan have gone. When I recently saw it in print, in a novel called *Letters from Constance* by Mary Hocking (London: Chatto & Windus, 1991), a story about a very English type of girl who marries a very Irish type of man, it struck me as strangely familiar until I remembered that it was a theory I had once developed myself, many years ago, when we first came to live in London. It is that the fairy folk live on in the Irish people who continue to live in Ireland. In one of her letters, Constance writes: 'I now believe in the Little People; they do not inhabit the mountains and glens, but live on in every Irishman.'

No sooner had we come to live in London than we – in common with many of the other Irish emigrants we met – began to think of those who had stayed on as slightly odd, certainly a little bit fey. They couldn't see it, and we could never have seen it ourselves until after we had left Ireland for good, but it's one reason why we could never go back there, and it could well be the reason why Irish people who emigrate and live their lives outside of Ireland are always known, when they go back, as 'returned empties'. The magic has gone out of them; they left it behind them, back in Ireland, when once the decision to emigrate was finally made.

If T. W. Rolleston is right, and the Milesians never existed, save in the minds of the early Christian scribes as a convenient way out of their dilemma concerning the descent of the saintly Irish Celts from sinful pagan gods and goddesses, and the Tuatha Danaan were in fact the final wave of Celts, only one single concrete artefact seems to have survived intact from that period to the present day: the Lia Fail (the Stone of Destiny) on which the High Kings of Ireland always stood during the coronation ceremony at Tara. The stone is said to have confirmed the election of a rightful monarch by roaring under him at the precise moment the crown was placed upon his head. The stone is believed to have been sent to Scotland from Tara early in the sixth century for the coronation of Fergus the Great, the son of Erc, who had begged his brother, Murtagh Mac Erc, then King of Ireland, to lend it to him to confirm the Scottish kingship for him, and it was never returned to Ireland.

It travelled down to London when King James VI of Scotland became King James I of Great Britain, at the time of the union of the Scottish and English Crowns in 1625, and it is still used at the coronation of English kings and queens in Westminster Abbey where it is now known as the Stone of Scone, although it seems to have stopped roaring long since. Today there is a standing stone on one of the hummocks at Tara, which are all that is left of the

Palace of Tara, and it is labelled the Lia Fail and indicates roughly where the original Lia Fail used to be situated during the coronation of the High Kings.

The Ulster cycle of sagas, which stars Cuchulain, contains many instances of interaction between the real, historical world and gods and fairies from the Other-world, the People of the Sidhe, formerly the Tuatha de Danaan. Cuchulain means the hound of Cullan, and he was given this name when, as a young boy called Setanta, he dallied playing hurling, and arriving late at a banquet at Cullan's house in Quelgny was attacked by Cullan's fierce wolfhound. The young boy Setanta killed the dog without any hesitation and without much bother, seizing the animal by the throat and flinging it against the gate-posts of Cullan's mansion. When he saw how bitterly his host grieved over the death of his faithful watchdog, the boy Setanta offered to guard Cullan's house himself against all comers until another wolfhound had been trained to take over the job, and so acquired the name by which he was known until his death.

Among the reappearing fairy folk was The Morrigan, one of the very few wicked members of the Danaan People, no less than a witch in fact. Morrigan – usually for some forgotten reason known as The Morrigan – was one of the Celtic goddesses of war, and she appeared to Cuchulain in the guise of a beautiful young maiden with traditionally welcoming thighs. When he rather uncharacteristically rejected her advances, she embarked on a campaign of persecution, on one occasion trying to drown him by turning herself into water-weeds and tangling herself around his feet.

And when, eventually, he was dying, mortally wounded after single-handedly defeating the entire army of Queen

Maeve of Connaught during the course of the Cattle Raid of Cuailgne (curiously spelled with a 'Q' in the Latin transcriptions of the old legends, though Saint Patrick's scribes later dropped the letter 'Q' when codifying Irish Gaelic) plus most of the men of Leinster and Connaught, chained to a standing stone so that he would at least die on his feet, The Morrigan came to him in the form of a crow, and perched on his shoulder to watch him die. There is a statue of Cuchulain, with The Morrigan perched on his shoulder, crystallised in bronze by the sculptor Oliver Shephard, in the General Post Office in Dublin, erected there to commemorate the Easter Rising of 1916.

The Hound of Cullan dies many times and in many different ways in the old Celtic myths and legends. In one, for example, as re-told by the poet W. B. Yeats in his verse play *On Baile's Strand*, he dies while attempting to do battle with the wild waves after slaying a son of his born to Aoife, a Scottish Celtic queen. He had never seen his son, but before the child was born he had placed a *geis*, or sacred vow, upon him never to reveal his identity to anybody, as a result of which the boy was unable to explain to his father who he was.

The Celtic sagas reach their apogee in the character of Cuchulain, the Hero of Erin, the Hound of Ulster, a man who would never acknowledge defeat, never surrender in any circumstances; and it is perhaps not insignificant that until the flight to the continent of the Ulster chieftains, the O'Neills and the O'Donnells of Tyrone and Donegal, after the defeat of the final attempt by the old Celtic aristocracy to break free from British dominion in Elizabethan times, Ulster remained the most fiercely Celtic – and, in a sense, the most republican – part of Ireland.

And even today, although the principal strain in Ulster Protestant blood is now that of the Presbyterian Lowland Scots (who were imported after the Flight of the Earls to re-populate the entire area with loyal servants of the Crown) there still seems to be enough of Cuchulain's genes left in the veins of the men of Ulster to make them the most formidable adversaries in all Ireland.

When a Southern Irishman says 'Not an inch', he means no more than four or five inches, and certainly not, at any rate, for the next five or six years or so. But when an Ulsterman says 'Not an inch', that's it: he means not the tiniest fraction of an inch, from now until the last syllable of recorded time. And when he says 'No Surrender' he means just that, no surrender, ever.

Which is one factor which has made what remains of the Irish Question so difficult to answer.

3

Island of Saints and Scholars

The Coming of Christianity

For over 1,100 years – that is to say over a period of time roughly equivalent to the interval between the high noon of Athens as the centre of Greek civilisation and the outbreak of the American War of Independence in the eighteenth century – the Irish Celts enjoyed a period of peace and prosperity unequalled anywhere else in the world. And this at a time when the barbarians – the Huns, Vandals, Goths and all those other savage tribes – came crowding out of eastern Europe to pull down and plunder one by one the outposts of the Roman Empire, and eventually, in 476 AD, to invade and sack the Roman capital.

After the last wave of Celts arrived in Ireland around 350 BC there were no further major invasions or incursions upon Irish territory until the first Viking long-boats slammed ashore on the Irish mainland and parties of fierce Scandinavian warriors started to ransack and loot the Christian monasteries, which by then had become the principal centres of population and wealth.

Any little cross-channel traffic that existed in the intervening period had mostly been in the other direction. The Celtic Irish kings and chieftains, always on the look-out for slaves to fetch and carry for them, were in the habit of sending raiding parties across the Irish Sea. This practice had begun long before the Romans invaded Britain and it continued throughout the four centuries during which Britain was a Roman colony. Nor did it stop when the legions of York, under Constantine, were withdrawn to Rome and subsequently decamped to the new capital and centre of the Roman Empire, the ancient city of Byzantium, at that time renamed Constantinople. It has, of course, since been renamed again, and is now known as Istanbul.

Towards the end of the reign of a Celtic High King known as Niall of the Nine Hostages (an ancestor, incidentally, of the O'Neills of Tyrone and through them, of Captain Terence O'Neill, later Lord O'Neill, the first Prime Minister of the state of Northern Ireland to set foot on Republican Irish soil), a Celtic Irish expeditionary force captured a mixed bag of Roman riff-raff which happened to include a young Welsh-born boy, a British Roman citizen called Patrick, the son of a local magistrate.

Patrick, kidnapped in Wales, spent his formative years as a slave, herding sheep on the slopes of a mountain called Slemish in County Antrim. In due course, he escaped from slavery and studied for the priesthood in France, where he worked with the famous Bishop Germain – subsequently Saint Germain – of Auxerre. He returned to Ireland in 432 AD, determined to preach

Christianity to the illiterate pagans among whom he had spent his youth.

He was not the first priest to attempt to do so. Before him there had been Isernius from Leinster, who had been a fellow-student of Patrick's at Auxerre, and Palladius, who had died just before Patrick arrived from Auxerre to assist him. But neither of them had made much impression on the defiantly pagan Irish Celts.

Even in his wildest dreams, Patrick could hardly have foreseen the fanatical zeal with which his former captors, the mystical and romantic Celts, would take to the bleak religion he preached. He began his mission by triumphantly destroying some idols in County Cavan, site of *Crom Cruach*, the chief and one of the few centres of idolatry in Ireland (the Celts had mainly worshipped invisible, spiritual gods who only took human form when it suited them), and before long he was visiting the court of High King Laoghaire, at Tara, and explaining the purpose of his visit to the assembled company. He proved persuasive enough to talk the High King's brother into allowing himself to be baptised and at Easter time in AD 433 – a time the Celts also celebrated, but as a festival connected with the sowing of seeds – King Laoghaire also pardoned Patrick for the offence of igniting a Paschal fire on a hill at Slane near Tara, before King Laoghaire had the official fire on Tara Hill. He even allowed Patrick to explain that he had broken the king's laws to commemorate the resurrection of Jesus Christ and boast that he had finally set alight a flame in Ireland which would never be extinguished.

One legend has it that he used the three-leafed Irish shamrock to illustrate the principle of the Trinity, though why something as basically simple as the Lesser Trefoil could in any way clarify the impenetrable mystery of the unitarian nature of the Father, the Son and the Holy Ghost has always escaped me. Another legend was that the shamrock would never grow in alien soil, though this is patently untrue; the Lesser Trefoil is as common over much of western Europe as it is in Ireland. Yet a third legend associated with Saint Patrick is that he banished the serpent from Ireland; it is true that snakes are very rarely found in Ireland – almost, but not altogether, never – but this may well be due to the fact that snakes are sensible creatures and prefer a more clement climate.

For almost thirty years, Patrick travelled the land surrounded by a retinue of officials, initially Bretons and French Celts, but increasingly replaced by Irish Celts who supervised the building of churches and monasteries. They instructed the Irish Celts in the rites of the Christian Church and taught them how to read and write, beginning with the task of copying out the catechism and the commandments.

Possibly because he was a Celt himself, Patrick did not attempt to persuade his converts to abandon altogether the heroes and heroines of their myths and legends, nor did he require them to revise all their ancient laws and practices. Instead, he helped them to draw up a new code of laws, excluding only those measures which were in violent opposition to the Christian code of conduct, and managed to find a middle ground which reconciled the ancient Irish Brehon laws (so called from the Irish word for judge) with those of Rome. He also cultivated in the Celts a great respect for Latin, then the universal European language of science and learning, and adapted the organisation of the Irish Church to the realities of the Irish situation. The Roman administration had been based on towns, but in Ireland there were no towns, only *communes* and townlands; so Patrick created bishoprics wherever he could find a local ruler whose authority was accepted by at least a few of the families living in his area or *tuath* – as the smaller tribal units were known – and within a few short years he had succeeded in creating more than 350 bishoprics.

The distinctive nature of Celtic civilisation, and the complete lack of urban communities or even of established political systems upon which some sort of a diocesan structure could be based, resulted in the development of a Christian organisation which differed fundamentally from the Roman pattern, a situation which was to cause a certain amount of trouble later.

But initially, it seemed to be working splendidly. Patrick and his early followers built in Ireland a church based on the monastic system. And the monasteries which they established remained the major centres of population and wealth in the country until the arrival of the Scandinavians.

His choice of Armagh, the former site of Emain Macha, the capital and centre of Cuchulain's world, for the episcopal primacy was also inspired; no choice could better have pleased the old Druidic *filidh*.

And Patrick's scribes, though they probably insisted on the insertion of the Christian version of the creation myth as a foreword to many of the Celtic sagas, appear to have shown as much sympathy as Patrick himself had evinced for the ancient Irish mythology, and even seem to have shared some of the pagan, Celtic reluctance to abandon altogether the old ideas. Certainly, they could hardly have believed that the inclusion of glimpses of the lusty old life of the Celtic gods and goddesses could possibly have assisted in any way the spread of the bland Christian concept of a Heaven in which the only diversion appeared to be the dubious delight of listening to sexless angels in long white flowing robes plucking at harps and singing hymns.

The Christian scribes, in their transcriptions of the Irish legends, even allowed Oisin, the fiercest fighter of all the Fianna, to query the advantages of the Christian heritage, and duly reported his answer in *Duanaire Finn*, edited and translated by Gerard Murphy for the Irish Texts Society in 1933 and quoted by Robert Jerome in *Irish History and Culture* (Kansas University Press, 1976).

Saint Patrick's scribes allowed Oisin to lament the passing of the old Celtic way of life: 'I would sooner at rising, hear grouse on mountain peaks, than the voice of the cleric indoors, bleating like a sheep or a goat ... No gathering, no music, no harps, no great bestowal of wealth, no deeds of horsemanship, no rewarding of the learned with gold, no art, no festive drinking ... No courting, no hunting, the two crafts most looked forward to, no fighting, no raiding, no learning of athletic feats ... time passes wearily in Elphin tonight.'

How the Christian scribes acquired such a close rapport with the ancient Celtic story-tellers is another matter. Indeed, it isn't even very clear how Roman scribes managed to pin down the basic elements of the Celtic language and literature.

Language is far more important than it appears at first glance. If you stop to think about it, even shallowly, it soon seems clear that man thinks in a form of language and dreams in words as well as in images. For example, when I am in England, I always dream in English, but after a couple of weeks in France, I invariably dream in

French. In fact, that is the sign that I have successfully made the transition. My conclusions on this subject are borne out by, among others, the currently fashionable Roddy Doyle who told John Ardagh that he wasn't interested in what things or people look like and went on: 'I see people in terms of dialogue and I believe that people are their talk.' Language also facilitates perception. Whatever the object, whether a Wonderbra or a flying buttress, if you happen to know the name for it, you are more likely to recognise it when you next encounter it.

In discussing it with people who know far more about the subject in general than I do, it seems likely that the early Latin scribes did their best to render the tales they had heard in spoken Irish Gaelic and tried to render it in writing, using Latin characters and Greek and Latin forms of grammatical construction. While doing this, they clearly found some of the Latin letters redundant (to use a modern phrase), but what is not nearly so clear is how they developed the distinctive Irish alphabet. Interestingly, Irish Gaelic is one of a series of Indo-European languages which includes Hellenic (Greek), Italic (the Italian languages), Celtic, Germanic, Baltic and Slavic.

As to how these primitive languages ever came to be written down, the Greeks are not a great help. They refused even to attempt to listen to people who spoke strange languages and disparagingly referred to them all as *barboroi*, or babblers, because they couldn't be bothered to try to understand what the barbarians, as they came to be known, were saying. Interestingly, the only alternative to the range of Indo-European languages at this period was the choice between two Afro-Asiatic ones: Arabic and Semitic, the latter bearing a very close resemblance both to today's Hebrew and Arabic.

But including highly derogatory material – derogatory, that is, of the Christian message – in their transcriptions of the legends, the early Irish Christian scribes themselves were clearly looking back nostalgically to some of the more attractive features of life in pre-Christian Ireland.

This cycle of Celtic tales ends with the final reconciliation of the old pagan values with the new Christian virtues. Patrick asks his guardian angels whether they think it would be all right with God for him to listen to all the pagan stories, and when they assure him that it would, he himself takes over the propagation of the Celtic Irish myths. Even Oisin, for all his deep doubts, was baptised in the end before he died, a victim of Saint Patrick's charm, as equally undoubtedly, Saint Patrick had been a victim of his . . .

And while there doesn't seem to be much doubt that Saint Patrick was flexible enough to bend the rules and regulations of Christianity to meet the circumstances as he found them, on the ground, in Celtic Ireland over 1,500 years ago, it has also been suggested (most recently by John Minahane in *The Christian Druids*, Sanas Press, 1994) that the Druids were equally tolerant and actually facilitated, rather than opposed, the advance of Christianity.

On the face of it, this seems absurd. The Druids, a powerful secretive élite, had everything to lose and nothing to gain by assisting Saint Patrick in his mission. And indeed, all the evidence points the other way. It was Christianity which caved in, in Ireland, to the old primitive beliefs and customs; to the extent, even, that polygamy was accepted as a way of life until around the end of the twelfth century. Also, because perhaps of a race memory of formidable fighting females like Queen Maeve, women were granted a much higher status in the early Christian Irish communities than they were elsewhere in Christendom, where the views of Saint Paul, rather than those of Saint Patrick, tended to prevail.

This accommodation by the Catholic Church of earlier, pagan deities was by no means confined to Ireland, incidentally. In Brittany, the Catholic Church at first fought bitterly against local superstition and magic, the whole basis of the Breton religion, but in the end was forced to incorporate into the Breton version of Christianity magic fountains and even fairies, regarded by the Bretons as 'delicious forbidden fruit'. Many of the villages in Brittany are named after saints who were survivors of pagan divinities, which were reluctantly accepted by the Church, and continued to perform the traditional functions (curing dropsy or ulcers, or finding missing objects) that they had always performed for their Breton adherents.

The great monasteries set up by Saint Patrick's disciples and successors – such as Glendalough, not far from Dublin, founded by Saint Kevin, and Clonmacnoise, on the Shannon, founded by Saint Ciaran – were famous centres of culture and learning at a period when the rest of Christendom was stumbling about aimlessly, caught up in the long nightmare of the Dark Ages.

The rest of Christendom with the exception, perhaps, of its principal headquarters. In Rome, the church and its bishop had survived all the invasions and upheavals which had led to the final dissolution of the Roman Empire. For twelve generations, Rome had been overrun by tribes of barbarians, pushed down into the old territories of the Empire by the invasion of Europe by the Huns. For over two centuries they had been busy plundering the palaces, wrecking the roads and bridges, burning down the public buildings and reducing the centre of civilisation to a benighted wilderness in which war, rape, murder and arson were daily occurrences, and only the Roman Church could claim any sort of continuity with the past.

When the barbaric successors of the Roman emperors started to quarrel among themselves, it became relatively easy for the more politically sophisticated bishops of Rome to maintain and reinforce what they now looked upon as their own city-state, and before long, a few pathetic remnants of the great Roman Empire, scattered throughout the peninsula of Italy, came to accept the bishops of Rome as their political as well as their spiritual rulers.

For although the Roman Empire was now clearly at an end, the concept of an empire based on Rome remained firmly fixed in men's minds; it was, after all, the only order they had ever known about, in a world grown increasingly disorderly. And, in the absence of any other candidate with any more cogent claim to continuity, the Church of Rome was gradually accepted as the principal temporal power in that area, as well as the supreme spiritual one, and the bishops of Rome, who had adopted the title of Pontifex Maximus, the most ancient of all the titles which the old Roman emperors had enjoyed, took over from them.

With the exception of the Anglo-Saxons, who had replaced the Roman provincials in Britain and who continued to govern themselves as they had previously done in the lands from which they had come, the Germanic invaders did not impose any of their own political institutions upon the remnants of the Roman

Empire, but lived alongside the old Roman population in circumstances more or less the same as those before the Roman Empire collapsed, though it was now the Church which ran the empire. Eventually, in AD 962, following a dubious deal between Otto I – the most formidable of the Teutonic barbarian leaders of Western Europe after the death of Charlemagne – and Pope John XII, the Holy Roman Empire of the German Nation appeared on the scene, a highly unlikely outfit which survived until 1806.

It was also very largely due to the Church's influence that, except in Germany and Britain, the Germanic tribes which settled in the former Roman territories in Europe adopted variants of the Latin language in place of their own tongues; French, Italian, Spanish and Portuguese all grew out of Latin, and survived in a written form as a result of the efforts of the Church. The Church also provided the only schools in existence and fostered such learning as there was; it is no coincidence that the words for clerk and cleric are the same or similar in many European languages.

Under the monastic form of management developed by Patrick and his successors, and cut off as it was from any regular contact with Rome by the Anglo-Saxon island intervening, the Irish Church developed along quite different lines from the diocesan Roman pattern, and was governed and directed far more by the abbots and the regular clergy in the monasteries than by the cathedral chapters and the parish priests.

The monasteries, right from the beginning, were not only great centres of learning and culture, but in the absence of any towns or cities they also soon became the centres of much of the social, commercial and intellectual life of the country. From these monasteries, Patrick's successors set out first as pilgrims, and then as missionaries, determined to rekindle the flame of Christianity first in Britain, and then all over the continent, not that it had ever completely disappeared.

During the darkest days of the Dark Ages in Europe, the tiny island of Ireland became an ecclesiastical centre of culture and learning that was known throughout the continent. Irish monks were in great demand as scribes and translators all over Europe, and Irish craftsmen and artists were renowned for the high quality of their products, disseminated by the missionaries.

One of the first great missionaries was Saint Columba, a descendant of the High King, Niall of the Nine Hostages, who established a colony on the island of Iona in AD 563, off the west coast of Scotland, from which he proceeded to convert Scotland to Christianity. Later, another monk, Saint Aiden, established an Irish Christian colony on the island of Lindisfarne off the Northumberland coast, which became for many years the centre of the Christian Church in England. Other Irish monks fanned out across the continent: Saint Fursey to Peronne in the north of France; Saint Kilian, to Wurzburg in Germany; Saint Vergil to Salzburg in Austria; Saint Columbanus to Bobbio in Italy and Saint Gall, who founded fifty religious houses in Switzerland as well as the town that still bears his name: and they all spread the name and fame of the Island of Saints and Scholars as well as the Word of God.

But, as the Catholic Church steadily increased its hold on temporal things in Europe, the Irish Church's isolation from developments in Rome began to be noticed. In 567, the Pope sent a mission of his own to re-convert England under Saint Augustine, who established his headquarters at Canterbury, just as Patrick had at Armagh, and founded diocesan centres at St Albans, Winchester and York. One of his followers, Wilfred, Abbot of Ripon, challenged the path that the Irish Church had taken at the great synod at Whitby in 664, and forced the Irish Church to conform more closely to the diocesan pattern established by Rome; thereafter the Church in England began to take its lead from Canterbury, rather than Lindisfarne.

The Vikings made their first attack on Ireland in 831, landing in the estuaries of the Shannon and the Bann, and from the latter taking possession of Armagh, headquarters of Saint Patrick's Church. The first attempted invasion efforts were resisted, as the Irish Celts rallied under High King Malachy but, in 852, the Vikings landed in force in Dublin Bay and established a fortress and headquarters which became a busy seaport and their principal city in Ireland. Later waves of Vikings built harbour fortresses which became Ireland's other major seaports – Wexford, Waterford, Cork, and Limerick among them. Only in Ulster did the strength of the O'Neill dynasty prove strong enough to prevent the Vikings from building any ports or cities in northern Ireland.

For nearly two hundred years the Danes occupied large areas of Ireland, mostly along the coastline near the natural harbours. They pillaged the monastic settlements and exacted tributes in return for undertakings not to plunder, a primitive version of today's protection racket. The Irish kings, as usual, were far too busy quarrelling among themselves to make any concerted effort to get rid of them. It was during this period that the monks started to build those tall round towers peculiar to Irish ecclesiastical architecture. Whenever another wave of Vikings arrived, they would retire into these towers, pull up the ladders, and continue their task of writing down all the old Celtic myths and legends.

However, around the year AD 1000 a sort of uneasy unity was eventually achieved by a king called Brian Boru who became, if only very briefly, the first undisputed native Christian king of a united Ireland. Under his regime some of the damage done to the religious establishments was repaired and the country began again to enjoy for a time a measure of peace and prosperity. The Danes, though defeated in battle, were allowed to retain their seaport settlements – the trade they had built up was proving quite useful to the Celtic kings – though they now, in their turn, had to pay tributes. Many of the Viking warriors took Celtic maidens as wives and mistresses and the hitherto pure Celtic Irish strain received the first of many alien traces that were to dilute and diversify it over the centuries.

Inevitably, the Danes regrouped their forces and the final showdown came on the seashore at Clontarf, just outside Dublin, in 1014. After an epic battle that lasted from dawn until sunset, the Danes were driven into the sea, and lost 7,000 men. One of the Irish casualties in the battle was King Brian Boru, killed in his tent at the age of seventy-four. Needless to say, there were Irish troops fighting on the Danish side, notably the men of Leinster who resented Brian Boru's attempt to dominate all Ireland.

So the Irish once again had control of their own affairs, but only for a mere 150 years. During this time the restoration of the monasteries and seats of learning which had been started by Brian Boru was continued by his successor Malachy, and by a namesake of his, a young priest who was to become Archbishop of Armagh and ultimately a saint; he was also responsible for a revised ecclesiastical division of Ireland, which persists to the present day.

By this time, other parties of Vikings who had landed in France, and found it greatly to their liking, had settled there in the area now known as Normandy and had become the Normans. And it was as the Normans that they invaded England in 1066, defeated the Anglo-Saxons, took over the country and became the Anglo-Normans, who in turn became the English, and then in turn the imperial and imperious British.

By this time, too, complaints about the continuing non-conformity of the Irish Church were beginning to reach Rome. And apart from the irregularity of the Irish Church structure, there was the point that Ireland, alone of all the Christian countries, had so far contributed no troops to the crusades against the Moslems. As early as 1159, the Pope – the first and only English pope, Nicholas Breakspeare – published a bull, as papal edicts were known, bestowing the island of Ireland upon the Anglo-Norman king, Henry II, in the mistaken belief that a short spell of firm Anglo-Norman rule would soon bring the wayward Irish Church and its Celtic adherents to heel.

The repercussions of that decision are still all around us.

4

Prisoners of the Past

Irish History

The English can never understand why everything that happens in Ireland seems to be connected with ancient history, nor why Irish people seem to be imprisoned in their own past.

In this connection, there is a story, and so far I haven't been able to trace it, though it doesn't matter whether it's true or not, or whether the source can be traced, because it embodies a certain essential truth: if it didn't happen in fact, it easily could have happened.

It concerns Eamon de Valera and David Lloyd George, in 1921, when the two of them got together for the first time to discuss possible solutions to the Irish Question. After they'd been at it, hammer and tongs, for a whole day, Lloyd George gave a press conference in the evening, and was asked by the British journalists how it had gone. 'Mr de Valera has been talking non-stop since eight o'clock this morning,' Lloyd George told the journalists, 'filling me in on the background to the Irish fight for freedom. And after eight hours and sixteen minutes, he hasn't even reached the Norman invasion of Ireland yet.'

So, let's try to get shut of all that you really need to know about Irish history in just a few pages.

Apart from the fact that during the Roman occupation of Britain, a relatively small number of Irish Celts moved across the water to Scotland – from where the early Irish Stone Age men had originally come – and became the *Scotiae*, as the Romans called them, Ireland's only colonial connections had always been, so to speak, at the receiving end. There was a brief renaissance in the eleventh and twelfth centuries as the monasteries were rebuilt and repaired after the Viking depredations, and the arts and crafts began to flourish once more before the arrival of the Anglo-Normans. And it is worth noting that Ireland became an Anglo-Norman colony, not as a consequence of any covetous, conquering zeal on the part of England's monarchs, but as a direct result of Irish disunity, the cause of so many Celtic calamities, before and since.

Towards the end of the twelfth century, England's Norman barons, always on the look-out for fresh lands to conquer and new raw materials for their armies, may have been starting to consider the possibilities offered by their undeveloped next-door neighbour, Ireland, but the initiative did not come from them. And although their King, Henry II, had been urged by the Pope as early as 1159 to take possession of Ireland in order to bring it more into line with the rest of Christendom, Henry hadn't got around even to thinking about it when, in 1168, the Celtic King of Munster, Dermot MacMurrough, defeated and banished by the High King Rory O'Connor, and determined to avenge himself, travelled to Bristol to enlist an army of Norman auxiliaries to help him win back his kingdom.

Dermot brought his beautiful daughter Aoife, or Eve, with him to Britain and offered her hand in marriage, with the additional bonus of the kingship of Leinster, to any Anglo-Norman baron prepared to lead such an expeditionary force. He could afford to make this offer because he was planning, with the help of the Norman troops, to take over the High Kingship of Ireland himself.

A small Norman expeditionary reconnaissance force landed at Baginbeg Head in County Wexford on 1 May 1169, to be followed in August 1170 by two hundred mounted knights in armour and some thousands of foot soldiers under a Norman baron, the Earl of Pembroke, who had lived in Wales and was known as Strongbow. He conquered Waterford and Dublin without much bother, and on the strength of his marriage to Dermot MacMurrough's daughter, adopted the title of King of Leinster. And he was just settling in, preparatory perhaps to breaking away from England altogether and setting up his own independent Norman kingdom in Ireland, when Henry II landed unexpectedly with a huge army of five hundred knights, three or four thousand archers and enough arms and equipment to put Strongbow firmly in his place.

As soon as he had established himself in Dublin, in a wooden castle just outside the Viking walls of the city, Henry II started to hold court, to assert his authority and to receive and entertain his new 'subjects' – who included many of the Celtic Irish kings and chieftains with their retinues – from November to March, interestingly the traditional Dublin Castle 'season' of balls, soirées and levees, which survived until the British finally pulled out of Southern Ireland about 750 years later.

Eventually, disregarding the High King and all Irish notions of sovereignty and land ownership, Henry declared himself overlord of Ireland and proceeded to parcel up the island between various of his Norman knights and the few provincial kings and chieftains who could be persuaded to agree to pay an annual tribute to him.

When he returned to England in April 1172, he left behind him a handful of barons and an army of knights and archers who now began to spread their power piecemeal, attempting to reproduce in Ireland the whole Norman feudal structure of manors and abbeys, castles and fortresses. In time, their presence there came to be accepted by the Celts; and the Normans, for their part, began to adopt some of the easy-going and casual Irish habits and customs, becoming in the much-quoted phrase that is probably more memorable than it is accurate, 'more Irish than the Irish themselves'.

Left to their own devices, the Anglo-Norman colonists would probably, like Saint Patrick before them, have found some way of adapting their laws and customs to make them more acceptable to the Celts and their system of land-ownership, but their monarchs insisted on forcing them to ignore all Irish traditions and to run Ireland as a feudal Anglo-Norman colony.

Before very long, many second- and third-generation Anglo-Norman lords, born and brought up in Ireland, began to regard themselves not as Anglo-Norman, but as Anglo-Irish, a situation which didn't at all appeal to the English kings, who greatly feared a line-up between these Anglo-Irish barons and the ancient Celtic kings and chieftains.

Ireland's first Parliament was appointed, not elected, towards the end of the thirteenth century; its members were chosen from the ranks of the archbishops, bishops, abbots and priors, and from those of the barons, nobles and knights. The official language of the Parliament was French – no Celts were present, except among the clergy – and one of its first actions was to draw up a series of decrees designed to discourage the colonists from assimilating in any way with the natives.

It needed only the Reformation to add the disastrously divisive element of religious bigotry to the gulf which had by now been successfully created between the Celtic Irish and their Anglo-Norman overlords. What had previously been only a fundamental difference in race and outlook flared into a fanatical hatred when Henry VIII – and, to a much greater extent, his successors – tried to impose the customs and practices of the new, reformed religion on the Celtic Catholic Irish.

The Reformation also added greatly to the Crown's problems with the Anglo-Norman overlords, many of whom disliked the religious changes every bit as much as the Irish did, and tended to side with the Irish against the Crown. Aware of this, and aware, too, that he could no longer continue to claim to be holding the country on the Pope's behalf, since he had so signally failed to acknowledge the Pontiff's authority in other matters, notably in relation to his own marital affairs, Henry VIII had the title King of Ireland conferred upon him by edict of the Irish Parliament. He also forced the lords and barons and Irish chieftains who had held titles under the old regime to surrender their lands to him and receive them back, to be held under the system of knight-service. Some of the old Celtic chieftains were thus given English titles, which explains why the O'Neills of Ulster, descendants of the ancient Celtic High King Niall, came to hold the English title of Earls of Tyrone.

The stage was now set for a series of rebellions and uprisings, as often as not planned and led by members of the Anglo-Norman Ascendancy, many of whom had become Anglo-Irish rather than English in their sympathies. Sometimes these were supported by expeditionary forces sent by continental countries anxious for one reason or another to have a crack at Protestant England, and they were usually followed by vast confiscations of land still in Irish hands, which was then repopulated with loyal English or Scottish settlers, or awarded to the soldiers who had helped to put down the rebellions.

The last stand of the old Celtic Catholic aristocracy took place in Ulster where the O'Neills of Tyrone and the O'Donnells of Tyrconnell (Donegal) held out for nine years against Elizabeth's forces, with the support of some Spanish troops and the Irish armies of Gaelic Celtic chieftains from all over the country. When they had been finally defeated, and then pardoned and reinstated in their lands, the O'Neills and O'Donnells bought a ship and cleared out of Ireland for good, taking with them into exile on the continent ninety-eight of the other Celtic Catholic chieftains.

This Flight of the Earls, as it was called, was held to be treason; all their lands were confiscated, and the entire area was re-planted with loyal Scottish Lowland Presbyterians and stout English Protestant yeomen. And it was the introduction of these alien settlers, utterly different from the Celtic Catholic Irish in background, race and religion, and all concentrated in one corner of the country, which laid the foundation for the partition of the country three hundred years later, as well as for all the troubles in Northern Ireland during the past twenty-five years.

Another Protestant-Catholic war broke out in 1641, during which the new Protestant settlers were subjected to some terrible acts of reprisal. And, although the main motive behind the atrocities was the anger of the Irish at having been deprived of their lands, and was not primarily religious, much of the Protestant Ulsterman's deep distrust of what he always calls 'Roman' Catholics stems from this period.

Eventually the last smouldering remnants of the rebellion were stamped out with zealous efficiency and terrible cruelty during an invasion by Cromwell's Parliamentary Army in 1649; and it was followed by a new policy of clearing as many Catholics as possible out of the other three provinces and herding them all into the harsh and barren wilderness of Connemara, west of the Shannon river.

Things began to look a bit more hopeful when a Catholic king, James II, came to the English throne, but he didn't last very long, and when King William of Orange landed in England in 1688 to secure forever the Protestant succession, James fled first to France and thence to Ireland to raise a Catholic army, in a desperate effort to regain his throne. William followed him over with an army of 36,000 men, and, naturally enough, the recently-imported Scots Presbyterians and English Protestants in Ulster rallied to support him, and James II and his Catholic army were decisively defeated at the Battle of the Boyne in 1690.

In 1795 and again in 1798, a society called the United

Irishmen, strongly influenced by the French Revolution, and led by a Protestant Ulster lawyer, Wolfe Tone, and one of the old Anglo-Irish aristocrats, Lord Edward Fitzgerald, with some half-hearted French assistance, made efforts at an insurrection which was quickly quelled. Then, in 1803, a Dublin Protestant called Robert Emmet and a tiny band of fanatical followers tried to seize Dublin Castle in the most pathetic attempt at a rebellion of them all. The only concrete result of the whole affair was the killing, in the confusion, of an elderly and well-intentioned judge. Emmet was hanged, but not before he had made a speech from the dock which was to keep the spirit of rebellion alive for another generation. 'When my country takes her place among the nations of the world,' he said, 'then, and not until then, let my epitaph be written.'

From 1800, Ireland was ruled directly from Westminster – much as Northern Ireland is now – with 100 (later 105) Irish MPs sitting at Westminster. After a Land War during the course of which the Irish tenant farmers became peasant proprietors, paying annuities instead of rent to the British Government to recompense Britain for buying out the absentee Anglo-Irish landlords, the Irish Nationalist MPs had, by 1913, very nearly succeeded in achieving Home Rule, when the Protestant Ulster settlers formed a volunteer force to take arms and fight the forces of the United Kingdom if need be, in order to remain a part of it, rather than be obliged to become part of a Catholic Irish Free State.

The Irish Nationalists understandably retaliated by forming the Irish Volunteers, which became part of an Irish Republican Army that took over the General Post Office and other strategic buildings during the Easter

Rising of 1916, and held out against the British forces for nearly a week.

The fifteen executions which followed swung public opinion over to the Irish Republican movement, known as Sinn Fein (the words simply mean Ourselves, though with a slight, emphatic overtone, like *nous-mêmes* in French) though it took a terrible guerrilla war which dragged on until the summer of 1920 before the British finally caved in. And even then, the British Prime Minister, David Lloyd George, allowed the Ulster Unionists to pressure him into partitioning off six of the predominantly Protestant counties of Ulster into a separate statelet, Northern Ireland. This led to a disastrous civil war in the south, sporadic unrest in Ulster ever since, and the state of affairs, close to civil war at times, which has gone on in Northern Ireland from 1969 until the late summer of 1995.

After seven hundred years, Ireland was no longer a British colony, though it was not yet a nation. Not really a nation once again, as the old patriotic ballad put it, and not really free either, but nearly a nation once again, and very nearly free. The twenty-six counties of what was initially known as the Irish Free State, and is now the Republic of Ireland, succeeded in breaking all the remaining ties with the British monarchy by 1949, and joined the European Community as a separate nation, enjoying more or less the same status as the United Kingdom, in 1973.

Northern Ireland had a separate parliament from 1921, though the state was also represented by a dozen MPs sitting at Westminster, until, after repeated efforts on the part of the British Government to force both it and the local government authorities in Northern Ireland to give the one-third minority of Catholic Nationalists in their area a fair crack of the whip had dismally failed, it was prorogued and Northern Ireland is now, as the whole of Ireland was until the outbreak of the First World War, ruled from Westminster by a Secretary of State, chosen from and answerable to the British Parliament.

5

Water, Water, Everywhere

Natural Resources

When the shooting stopped, and the clouds of smoke began to drift away, after a rebellion followed by a period of martial law, followed by a protracted guerrilla war of independence, followed by a civil war (settled, incidentally by a dumping and not a general surrender of arms), a mixed bag of ex-freedom fighters, some formerly farmers, teachers, clerks, blacksmiths, lawyers and students, who together constituted all that was left of the legitimate government of the Irish Free State, sat down to survey the property they had inherited. They cannot have found the prospect very encouraging.

Their brand-new Irish Free State consisted of 27,000 square miles (70,000 square kilometres) of sparsely inhabited and largely undeveloped land, three-quarters of it too mountainous or too boggy to cultivate with, so far as they then knew, no mineral resources, no developed sources of power, and no skilled labour force. Such management expertise as existed was largely British-orientated, and very wary of the new regime. The people as a whole were utterly exhausted and demoralised by the troubles and, above all, by the desperate disillusions of the Civil War; and the economy had been run down by successive British governments, and was now, after over five years of turmoil, virtually at a standstill. Outside of the Six Counties of Northern Ireland, now partitioned off, there were almost no industries and practically all manufactured goods had to be imported. Finally, the entire country was physically in a mess: the roads and railways pitted with bomb craters; police and army barracks and public buildings of all sorts blown up or razed to the ground, fresh ruins everywhere to add to the ruins already so liberally strewn all over the Irish landscape over the centuries.

There was plenty of turf which could be burnt – just about – instead of coal. There were rivers to provide water and from which, in time, hydro-electricity might be produced. There was grass, acres and acres of it, on which cattle and horses could be raised. No forests to speak of; even wood was a costly imported luxury. Plenty of fish in the rivers and in the sea, but not many people disposed to take them out of it, except in pitifully small numbers, and not much of a market for it anyway. The Irish were never a great fish-eating people, possibly because as a result of the Catholic notion of abstaining from meat on a Friday, they felt that fish was somehow inferior to meat; or possibly because the only food they had to exist on during the Famine was seafood in the form of mussels and other crustacea which could be picked up on the rocky Atlantic coast; hence the latter came to be regarded as 'famine food'.

There were the mountains and lakes, the beaches and the rivers – some of the finest scenery in Europe concentrated into a conveniently small area – but almost no decent hotels on which to base a tourist industry, even if people could be persuaded to spend good money taking their holidays in a country where they were still liable to be shot, either deliberately, or by mistake.

The Industrial Revolution had passed Ireland by, very largely because outside of the city of Belfast and its surrounding hinterland, there had been no industries to revolutionise. The only industries in existence – apart from a few family businesses like those set up by the Guinness family who made stout and the Powers and the Jamesons who made whiskey – were small manufacturers operating largely in traditional sectors such as food products (like Jacob's biscuits, another family firm), and textiles for the home market.

Industries could possibly be established, in time, and given the necessary capital; but who would be rash enough to invest in Ireland after all that had happened? Most of the money in the country was still in the hands of what was left of the Anglo-Irish gentry, and they weren't likely to part with it to a Sinn Fein Catholic government. It was a pretty daunting prospect all round.

Traditionally, Ireland had always been predominantly agricultural, so the first thing the new government did was to look at what that offered in the way of a prosperous future for the new state. Then, as in the time of Cuchulain, cattle outnumbered people in Ireland by about three to one. So the economy would probably have to be, as it had always been, based largely on beef and dairy produce. This immediately posed them with an almost intractable problem: unemployment. Cattle-herding is the least labour-intensive industry in the world; one small boy with a stick can look after a whole herd of cattle. And before they could contemplate the development of any Irish industries, even on a small scale, those early Irish governments had first to come to grips with the realities of the power situation.

Because of its position in the path of the Gulf Stream, Ireland's climate is moist and temperate, so equable indeed that sub-tropical vegetation flourishes in the south-west corner of the island. But moist would be reckoned by many visitors to Ireland as a bit of an understatement. What the Irish always refer to affectionately as a soft day would be regarded by most people anywhere else as fairly wet weather, though there is a curious luminosity about the Irish mist that makes it unique: Yeats called it 'brightness falling from the air'.

When the weather is good in Ireland, it is very good indeed, and the landscape sparkles in some of the clearest, cleanest air in Europe, but the rain is never very far away. In Dublin Bay, they say that if you can see Howth Head clearly, it's going to rain, and if you can't see it clearly, it's already started to rain.

Irishmen don't take much water in their whiskey. They're deeply prejudiced against it, perhaps for the very good reason that there's far too much of it about. You can't get away from water in Ireland. No part of the island is farther than ninety miles from the sea, and most parts of it far less than that. There are lakes and rivers everywhere and the entire western seaboard is riven by fjords, estuaries and other inlets of the sea; it's impossible to find a corner of the country that doesn't feature a stretch of water of some kind, even if it's only a pool at the foot of a stack of turf or a puddle along the edge of a field.

Turf, or peat as it is known in England, Ireland's only indigenous fuel, apart from the remnants of the forests, is one by-product of this excess of water. Without water, there would be no turf. Unfortunately the converse is also the case. There is no turf without water. A bog in its natural state is about ninety-five per cent water.

It would be hard to imagine a less promising-looking fuel. It is a brown, spongy substance, composed of plant fibres that grew in and around lakes which dried up and disappeared centuries ago, broken down by the wind and the weather over thousands of years, and compressed into something that is a cross between a sod of clay and a chunk of tree bark. It doesn't look as if it would ever burn. A great deal of it will not in fact burn, though it will smoulder away sullenly, producing a vast amount of blue smoke with a pleasant heathery smell, plus a lot of whitish ash and a very small amount of very gentle heat. Only a race of people utterly devoid of coal, and very short on forests, would dream of attempting to burn it as fuel.

On the other hand, there is so much of it in the country, and so little else that you can do with it – you can't grow crops on it, or graze animals, or even build houses on a bog – that it is understandable that the Irish, over the years, have tried to get rid of some of it by burning it, though even that isn't easy. Indeed, until about thirty or forty years ago, the Irish used to stack the turf in the open air in the hope that the sun and wind would dry it out a bit and sometimes it did, and sometimes it didn't.

A devout Irish Christian – and most Irish people remained devout Christians from about AD 430 until the day before yesterday – might have wondered, during and after the Industrial Revolution, why it was that a nation so patently godless as the Brits should have been rewarded by the Almighty with a geological situation in which the remains of their primeval forests, compacted by the sheer weight of the centuries, should turn into coal, a fuel which burns so fiercely that it was capable of transforming the whole nature of civilisation within a century, while the faithful and devout Irish were saddled with forests and lakes which turned, not into coal, but into this sad and soggy stuff. In this, as in so many other matters, it didn't seem that the Almighty had been altogether fair to his most fervent followers.

More scientifically-minded fellow-countrymen would have known that all that turf is the result of yet another geological peculiarity: something to do with the effect of the retreating floes of the last Ice Age. But whatever the cause, the effect was the same: a pretty dismal prospect for a new state contemplating industrialisation, even on a small scale.

And those first governments of the Irish Free State were unable to contemplate industry other than in the form of factories established in the vague hope of making Ireland self-sufficient, if at all possible, in some basic consumer goods previously imported, principally from England. The small Irish factories set up as a result of this policy could only produce goods that looked, and usually were, inferior to the English imported equivalents, which were also widely and attractively advertised in the English newspapers and magazines which continued to be bought and read by the Irish who still preferred to pay a bit more for the superior imported goods. To discourage this tendency, those first governments imposed increasingly heavy tariffs on all imported goods. These tariffs did not, however, discourage the Irish public from buying the imported articles even at ever higher prices, though the tax on the imported articles did provide a very useful source of revenue. Indeed, it became their principal source of income, along with the existing revenue derived from the heavy taxes on drink and tobacco inherited from the British administration. And the factories were bound to fail, when you think about it, because even if the Irish consumers had been prepared to buy their products, which they weren't, the home market would still have been far too small to support them.

The provision of hydro-electric power from Ireland's rivers and lakes became a fairly urgent priority, and the first government of the Free State arranged with Siemens-Schukert, the German engineers, to design a system to damn the Shannon river at Killaloe at the foot of Lough Derg, to provide hydro-electric power for the new State. But the demand for electricity outstripped the supply even before the Shannon Scheme was completed and it was abundantly clear, as early as that, that hydro-electric power could never produce more than a small fraction of Ireland's energy requirements.

There was always the vague hope that reserves of oil or natural gas might be found on Irish territory or under the seas that surround the island, but until the discovery of some rich seams of natural gas in the sea off Kinsale in County Cork in 1973, the early governments were forced to face up to the fact that any industries that might be set up in Ireland would be almost entirely dependent on power produced from costly imported coal, or oil, or both.

Nor did Irish agriculture appear to be ready to lend

itself to development on an industrial scale or even very much in the way of basic mechanisation. The Land Wars of the late nineteenth century had been ended by a massive purchase by the British Government of land held by absentee landlords, mainly British. This land was broken up into small, hopelessly uneconomic holdings which were sold off to the tenant farmers who had formerly worked it. Not only were the holdings so uneconomically small that many of the new peasant proprietors were obliged to supplement the income from their farms by working on the roads for part of the year, but the Irish farmers were so suspicious of anything smacking of co-operative effort – communal ownership of agricultural machinery was seen as the thin end of the dreaded Communist wedge – and far too poor to buy tractors and farm machinery themselves, with the result that they were obliged to continue to work their farms using techniques and tools not much more advanced than those employed by the later Stone Age invaders of 6,000 years earlier.

All in all, it was not a very pleasing prospect.

Yet incredibly, by 1959, the year when Eamon de Valera – the last surviving Commandant of the 1916 Easter Rising – retired from politics to become President of Ireland, money had somehow been found to produce electricity from Ireland's rivers and turf bogs, to reclaim wastelands and build factories, to buy ships and aeroplanes, modern railway trains and motor buses, to nationalise the bloodstock trade and turn the breeding of race-horses into a lucrative export business, and to develop a thriving tourist industry which went a long way towards balancing the budget.

And by remaining neutral in 1939 in what was regarded in Ireland as Britain's war – although hundreds of thousands of Irish citizens joined up, many more in fact than those contributed by the still fiercely loyal northern state – the country had demonstrated to the world that it was finally and fully independent of Britain, and had earned the right to be taken seriously. Even seriously enough to attract foreign capital.

A couple of decades later what is widely known as Ireland's industrial miracle occurred. I don't propose to go into it in any detail here, because plenty of books have been written about it by a variety of authors, including my good self. It is probably enough to say here that from the late 1960s onwards, Ireland switched over from being an agricultural-based economy to an industrial one. Indeed between 1973 and 1983, Ireland's industrial exports increased by ten per cent per year, a rate of growth well in excess of the European Community and United States averages. By then industry was employing twenty-nine per cent of the total workforce, while those employed on the land had fallen from forty-three per cent in 1949 to seventeen per cent in 1983. This miracle was achieved by using whatever capital was available in various schemes designed to encourage foreign companies to set up factories in Ireland to manufacture goods there for export. Exports from Ireland during this period included articles as unlikely, in view of the country's earlier industrial history, as transistor radios and scientific instruments, silicon chips and other computer components, razor blades, pencils and sewing machines, pharmaceuticals and pianos, to customers as far apart as Norway and Switzerland, Panama and Soviet Russia, as well as Britain and the United States. Most important of all, perhaps, was that this industrial boom marked the end of Ireland's total dependence on Britain for its continued existence.

During the same period, agriculture was also thoroughly overhauled and modernised. Irish dairy produce was aggressively marketed worldwide, a sugar industry was set up utilising Irish beet which not only met the country's sugar requirements in full but also provided a healthy surplus for export to, among other countries, Britain. At one period Irish beef was feeding the British and American armies of the Rhine as well as both armies in the Iran-Iraq conflict.

What does all this prove? If anything, it proves that left to their own devices, and once they had finally succeeded in getting the British off their backs after seven hundred years, the Irish were perfectly capable of running their own affairs, and running them extremely efficiently. They were never cut out either to be a master race or a subject people; all they needed was a chance to run their own country in their own way, though the fact that that chance was denied to them for so long was largely due, among many other factors, to their own inherent disunity. But as soon as they managed to get their act together, they showed the world what they could do.

Saint Patrick, if he's still around anywhere, must be proud of his people, though a little sad, maybe, that his own favourite corner of his country still remains under alien management.

6

Small Farmers and Mohair Moguls

Agriculture and Industry

It is difficult to say whether the ancient Irish Celts were a rich or a poor people. Rich they certainly were, in terms of their flora and fauna and the beauty of the landscape in which they were lucky enough to be able to live out their lifespan, though the climate could have been a bit more clement. On the other hand, as few of them ever had the opportunity of venturing very far from the shores of their own windswept, wet little island, they had no way of knowing that the weather was any better anywhere else, so that shouldn't have troubled them overmuch. Nor would they have been a bit bothered by the fact that they didn't have any elaborate structures like the great ziggurat to the moon-goddess Su'en at Ur in Mesopotamia or the pyramids at Cheops in Egypt, and no great cities like Babylon or Nineveh or Persepolis or Alexandria, because they wouldn't have known anything about them, either.

Judged by contemporary Egyptian, Assyrian or Greek standards, the ancient Celts were probably paupers, but since they were completely unaware of that fact, they were exactly as rich as they felt themselves to be, which was very rich indeed. Certainly, there is no evidence in any of the old Celtic myths and legends that they ever considered themselves to be anything other than as good as the best of them. The national inferiority complex which clung to their descendants like a shroud until the late 1960s, and has since been completely and finally discarded by the current generation, probably didn't descend on the corporate Irish mind until some time in the nineteenth century. Throughout most of the seven hundred years of the Anglo-Norman and then the British domination, they mostly kept to themselves, spoke their own language, played their own music and danced their own dances, living out their own lifestyle, without worrying overmuch about wealth or possessions. It was only in the nineteenth century, when the Great Famine revealed how perilously close many of them were to starvation most of the time, that the Irish suddenly realised that they were among the poorest and most miserable people in Europe.

In the middle of the nineteenth century, what is now called a population explosion pushed the number of inhabitants in Ireland up beyond the eight million mark from about half that figure. Outside of the city of Belfast, most of the people had no source of livelihood other than the land, which naturally could not bear the ever-increasing pressure this population explosion imposed upon it, and the result, inevitably, was unemployment on a massive scale.

A Commission set up in 1836 to examine the problem

of unemployment in Ireland reported that the number of persons simultaneously requiring 'relief' during thirty weeks of that year was 2,385,000 out of a total population of eight million. Of those, 585,000 were unemployed men and the other 1,800,000 represented their dependants: wives and children, sisters and brothers, aged parents, uncles and aunts. More than half the entire population of the country lived on potatoes, or 'potatoes and point' – a piece of meat, suspended from a nail in the ceiling over the table, against which the potatoes were lightly brushed (pointed) to give them some semblance of flavour.

When a blight wiped out the entire potato crop in 1845 and again during the two following years, the Irish starved to death in their hovels and fields, or travelled, battened down in the holds of cargo ships, to the United States; between 1846 and 1851, more than one million Irish people died, and another 1,500,000 emigrated.

It is hard, nowadays, to understand how the failure of one single crop could have caused such widespread suffering. But you have only to drive through Connemara and look at the ruins of the hovels in which these peasants lived – some are still standing, in a land so boulder-strewn and barren that the fields are hatched with loose stone walls, built for no better reason than to get a few of the stones up off the soil so that something could be made to grow in it – to recognise that people prepared to live in conditions like these must have been so close to starvation at the best of times that the loss of a few drills of potatoes could easily have tipped the scale.

A few half-hearted attempts were made by the British administration and by various charities to help the Irish, but in the climate of a market economy, as fervently believed in then as it is today, although plenty of food was available in Ireland – indeed, during the Famine years more than 60,000 bushels of oats were shipped from the island – the starving Irish couldn't buy any of it because they had no money.

The Poor Law Guardians, Victorian workhouses, and the Protestant ethic of the deserving and the undeserving poor combined to underline and emphasise their abject poverty, and the frequent evictions for the non-payment of rents that had been racked up again and again by the agents of the absentee landlords aggravated the situation.

The pattern of Irish agriculture had already been set much earlier by the British overlords. The seventeenth- and eighteenth-century 'plantations' had uprooted many of the native Irish from their fertile farmlands in Ulster, Munster and Leinster, and had herded them into tiny, uneconomic holdings in Connaught, the least fertile part of the country and the most unsuitable for the sort of intensive market gardening that would be needed to make such small holdings viable.

The Penal Laws, by insisting that the lands of a Catholic must be split up, on his death, among all his sons, instead of being left to his eldest son, led to a proliferation of uneconomically small holdings. Then, after the plantations, agents who had been unable to entice English farmers to come over and work their new Irish lands in the more fertile areas were obliged to rent them out – again in hopelessly unviable small parcels – to the Irish, as tenant farmers.

The absentee landlords of the eighteenth and nineteenth centuries were interested only in getting the maximum return out of their land. They aggravated the problem further by discouraging the Irish tenant farmers from doing anything that would be likely to increase the productivity of their farms by racking up the rent at the first sign of any improvement. And one motive at least behind the endless evictions of the nineteenth century was the desire among landlords to clear all the small, unprofitable mixed farms off their estates and release the land for the far more profitable trade of cattle-ranching.

The Land War of the latter part of the nineteenth century was finally resolved by the purchase by the British Government of seven million acres from the mainly English, mainly absentee landlords. Using money raised by a public bond issue in London, the big estates were broken up and the land sold to the Irish farmers who had formerly worked it as tenants, at the very favourable price of £12 an acre, payable half-yearly over a period of about twenty years in a sort of mortgage arrangement known as the annuities.

This arrangement had the superficially desirable effect of transforming the Irish tenant farmers into peasant proprietors, but it did not, of course, solve any of their basic problems. Nor could it be expected that they would forget overnight the habits bred into them over the generations and start to plough some of their profits back into their holdings. All their instincts were to hold on grimly to the few acres they had managed to acquire, and any development which entailed an element of risk, even for the sake of long-term advantage, was instantly suspect.

When the nineteenth century drew to a close, the live cattle trade with Britain, and its resulting by-product, the dairy industry, were the mainstay of Irish agriculture. Ireland was selling more than seventy per cent of its agricultural produce to Britain, some of it at a loss, because of Britain's cheap food policy.

It was unfortunate that the co-operative movement, when it finally came, should have been started by a Unionist, Sir Horace Plunkett. This, added to the fact that he was also a Protestant and a landlord, immediately made the whole movement suspect. Then, during the Troubles, many of the thousand odd co-operative creameries which had already been established, and were just beginning to show their usefulness, were destroyed simply because of their Unionist connections. The mistrust of the co-operative movement persisted long after the foundation of the Irish Free State, and seriously hampered what should have been a natural and progressive agricultural development.

The new gentlemen farmers now owned the land they lived and worked on instead of farming it as tenants for landlords who had prospered because they had owned several dozen such farms, as well as hundreds of acres of cattle ranches which, too, had now been divided up into small holdings – but they soon found that they had to work on the roads for part of the year or go on the dole in order to augment the meagre income that their farms brought them.

When the Irish finally regained control of their own affairs in 1922, more than half of the working population was living off the land, either as small farmers or as farm labourers. The farmers rarely married until very late in their lives: they had to wait until both parents were dead, because they wouldn't inherit the farm until the father died, and they wouldn't dare bring a bride into the house so long as the mother was still there, ruling the roost, as Irish mothers tended to do. And when they did eventually marry, they immediately proceeded to father large families of nine or ten children who were destined to emigrate; even those who might have wanted to stay down on the farm couldn't, because the farms could not support them and none of the neighbouring farmers could afford to employ them.

Partly as a result of the early Irish governments' policies of self-sufficiency and de Valera's notions of frugal felicity, the farmers were never encouraged to invest in modern farm machinery, not that they would have done so, anyway. Farmers tend to be the most conservative people in the world and the Irish farmers were more conservative than most, and stoically accepted an almost medieval lifestyle – no electricity, no plumbing to speak of, no central heating, no comfort whatever to come home to after a long day spent up to their ankles in the soggy soil.

It was only after rural electrification brought first the radio and then the television into their homes that they realised what an enormous gap existed between their way of life and that of the city slickers, particularly after the industrial boom-time of the late 1960s brought in its train a very visible rash of new houses and bungalows, fast cars and smart caravans, luxurious wine bars, well-stocked supermarkets and lush shopping malls, fitted kitchens and jacuzzis and all the other appurtenances of the twentieth-century consumer society.

The flight from the land, first into the nearest town, then up to Dublin City, and finally over the water to England or even further afield, had by this time reduced the number of people living off the land in Ireland from over fifty per cent of the working population to well under thirty per cent, but this was still far higher than the figure in other developed European countries. Over the same period, the population of Dublin increased from less than half a million people to just over three-quarters of a million. Today, the population of Greater Dublin is well over one million – that's more than a third of the entire population of the Republic – and less than fourteen per cent of the working population live off the land. This figure, however, is still far too high – the highest in the European Union after Greece and Portugal; in the United Kingdom, only four per cent of the workforce lives off the land.

The fact that prices for farm produce, particularly meat, continued to rise after the end of the Second World War, prevented the flight from the land from reaching alarming proportions, though by that time even the miserably small amount of mechanisation that had been introduced to Irish farms meant that a fifty-acre farm which used to provide work for ten men now only required two or three; and by the early 1950s, up to 40,000 Irish men, women and children were emigrating every year, a figure that amounted to 1.5 per cent of the total population. If this had gone on at the same rate for another ten years, it would have reduced the already tiny population of Ireland by fifteen per cent and that at a time when the marriage rate was the lowest in the Western world; a state of affairs which led to some speculation as to whether Saint Patrick's people were not, in fact, a rapidly vanishing race.

The industrial and agricultural boom of the 1960s was partly based on the assumption that sooner, rather than later, Ireland and Britain would join the European Economic Community, as it was then called. In preparation for this, Irish farmers were actively encouraged by the Government to take out hefty loans to buy tractors and other farm machinery, to build barns and silos and outbuildings and to increase their production at whatever cost. In the climate of the period, most of them eagerly did so, and also took out further loans to transform their bleak abodes into something a bit more like the sort of homes they kept seeing on television and in the cinema.

It was widely believed that access to the Common Market would bring an immediate end to Britain's cheap food policy and secure realistic prices for Ireland's agricultural exports to Britain. And initially the Irish farmers did very well out of the Common Agricultural Policy, with its price guarantees and export subsidies, as well as out of the Structural, Regional and Social Funds of the EEC. Before long, however, over-production of agricultural produce, and particularly dairy produce, within the European Community led to the introduction of quotas, cut-backs and set-asides, and the creation of milk lakes, butter mountains and all those dead herds of intervention cattle.

It is not surprising that the farmers felt aggrieved at the 1992 CAP reforms and the 1993 GATT deal; they had been encouraged by successive governments to borrow large sums of money to increase production, only to be told, once they had succeeded, that European Community quotas prevented them from expanding further in an effort to pay back some of the money they had borrowed.

Recent governments have been trying to encourage the older farmers to retire and the younger ones to diversify into such fringe activities as forestry, pony trekking, farmhouse holidays, bed and breakfast, and other forms of what John Ardagh describes as 'agri-tourism' (in *Ireland and the Irish*, London: Hamish Hamilton, 1994), as well as into market gardening, particularly of organic vegetables and even the cultivation of mushrooms and selected market garden vegetable produce for the British market. Many wives of small farmers, who used to work on the farm on a full-time basis, have taken other jobs, in the local pub or hotel, or working in an office in the nearest town. A great many farmers in the west and south-west of Ireland are on a form of Income Support, widely known as the 'farmers' dole', which allows them to derive whatever earnings they can manage to get from the farm, and top their earnings up to the level of the ordinary dole, on a means test basis.

Farming is still Ireland's major industry, accounting for forty-two per cent of all foreign earnings, but most of this output (much of it in the form of processed food) comes from a small number of industrialised, highly efficient farms in the south and south-east. And the total number of farms has dropped dramatically, from just over 250,000 in the mid-1920s, in the early days of the Free State, to well under 120,000 today.

Among the non-farming population of Ireland, that is to say, eighty-six per cent of the total, the main concern is unemployment. Most of the new industries created in the industrial boom of the 1960s and 1970s – and since then, as a result of Ireland's access to the European Union – are high-tech industries, such as pharmaceuticals, computer components and software, which are not labour-intensive.

Most of the factories in Ireland are brand-new and highly automated and the continued installation of ever more high-tech manufacturing methods, mainly computer-controlled, has led to increasing lay-offs, and this at a time of recession in the United Kingdom, the United

States and Australia, with the result that not only can emigration no longer disguise the extent of the Irish unemployment problem, but also some of the former emigrants are starting to come home again, because by the early 1990s the social benefits available in Ireland had become as good as, if not better than, those available in Britain. Added to that, thousands of farm workers, rendered redundant by increasing agricultural mechanisation, have now come crowding into Dublin looking for work, and have added to the total number of unemployed in the city; previously, so long as they stayed down on the farm, they appeared in the statistics as 'self-employed', and did nothing to swell the statistical ranks of the unemployed.

By 1994, Ireland had the highest proportion of unemployed, in relation to the working population, of any state in the European Union. That this did not lead to any marked social unrest might be due to the fact that the basic unemployment benefit in Ireland is now about £60 a week, rising to about £130 if the claimant has a wife and a couple of kids, which is as much as most unskilled Irish workers could hope to earn even if they were in a steady job. So about thirty-five per cent of the workforce have reconciled themselves to a way of life built around the dole queue and watching video films on the television.

The large-scale unemployment, particularly among young people just out of school, has led to a wave of minor crime: burglary, particularly thefts from cars, bag-snatching, mugging, theft and the hi-jacking of motor cars and shoplifting. It has also led to widespread and massive drug abuse, which in turn has led to a big increase in more serious crimes, most of them drug-related. Ireland has as high a proportion of certified HIV-positive sufferers as any other state in the European Union. In Ireland the primary cause is generally believed to be the widespread use of infected needles, rather than an excess of either homosexual or heterosexual activities, though these have clearly been on the increase, too.

All these circumstances have combined to produce a particularly gruesome form of 'hold-up', in which the weapon is a hypodermic syringe contaminated with the HIV virus, and the price, for the man who refuses to hand over the goods, is not a bullet through the heart, but the prospect of a long and lingering death from Aids.

Those lucky enough to have jobs seem relatively content. Wages in Ireland now compare fairly favourably with the average wage in the United Kingdom. A top civil servant with the added amenities of security and a generous pension can earn up to £50,000 a year, and most young Irish men and women tend to go into jobs rather than try to start up in business on their own. This means that the majority of them are on PAYE – the pay-as-you-earn system of taxation evolved in Britain, by which tax is deducted at source, by the employer – and consequently are more susceptible to variations in the taxation patterns than freelance or other self-employed people. And those workers who are lucky enough to find themselves with some disposable income with which to play are far more likely to invest their spare cash in stray property deals, tickets for the National Lottery, or on a bet on the last race at Fairyhouse, than to dabble in stocks and shares, though there is some evidence of the rise of a new breed of Irish 'yuppies' – what author Tim Pat Coogan refers to as the 'mohair brigade'.

Taxes in Ireland are very high, among the highest in the European Union. This is partly because the Irish have always tried to match the living standards and welfare benefits of their generally better-heeled English neighbours, but it is also partly because much of the burden of the tax holidays, low corporation tax and other inducements offered in the 1960s and 1970s to encourage foreign industrialists to set up factories in Ireland, has, in the end, to be funded by the Irish tax-payers.

For a married couple, the first £6,000 of their earnings are tax-free, and child allowances could bring that figure up to £9,000 for a family with five children. After that it starts to escalate sharply. The standard rate is twenty-seven per cent, but the top level of forty-eight per cent is soon reached at £13,000, the salary of a junior secretary still in her first job in London. And if you include the 'voluntary' – a sort of state-sponsored BUPA for people earning too much to qualify for the free, means-tested NHS-type medicare – and other levies of all sorts, including VAT on almost everything, a lot of people who earn more than £13,000 a year are paying more than fifty-five per cent of their total salaries in tax, and a married couple with joint earnings of £21,000 would soon find themselves in the top tax bracket.

Value Added Tax (VAT) has always been very high in Ireland, although it was reduced from twenty-five per cent to twenty-one per cent in 1989 in line with European Union harmonisation plans. And a still higher basic tax of fifty-eight pence in the Irish punt, plus a Wealth Tax on all sums over £100,000, were introduced in 1978, but were removed a couple of years later, as was a property tax imposed in the 1970s. Then there was Deposit Interest Retention Tax (DIRT), a tax which hit the savers as it was levied directly on interest accrued in banks and building societies by long-term deposits, introduced in the 1980s.

On top of that, according to a table of comparative European Union taxes in *The Times*, following the 1994 Budget, the Irish pay about a £1 more for a litre of cheap table wine than the British, and nearly £3 more than the Italians and Greeks. They also pay more than fifty pence more for a litre of cheap beer than the British, and £1 more than the Spanish, Germans, Greeks and Luxembourgers. In general, the cost of living is about twenty per cent higher than it is in Britain. Petrol, cars and telephones are all far more expensive, as well as most food and drink, and clothes cost about the same. Houses are cheaper but according to the Organisation for Economic Co-operation and Development (OECD), Ireland comes second-last among all the other states of the European Community in terms of per capita private consumption, second-last as regards the number of cars per thousand members of the population (278 per 1,000 as against 181 in Portugal and 449 in the United Kingdom), and second lowest, again after Portugal, in the number of telephones per thousand members of the population (278 as against 181 in Portugal and 449 in the United Kingdom).

But, due very largely to the efforts of one man, Charles Haughey – known as 'The Boss', who was Taoiseach off and on during the 1980s – writers and artists once again enjoy the modern equivalent of the patronage which was once extended to the *filidh* and other wise men by the High Kings of Tara, and by all the other local kings and chieftains in the old Celtic aristocracy right up until the time of the Flight of the Earls and the collapse of the last of the great Irish Celtic families in the sixteenth century.

When he was Minister for Finance in 1969, Haughey introduced a scheme which made all earnings from 'creative' work free of income tax for Irish and foreign writers and artists living in Ireland. If by doing so, he hoped to turn Ireland into a tax haven to which all the leading poets, painters, composers, novelists and other writers from all over the world would come flocking and turn it into a new Renaissance Florence, he was sorely disappointed. A few writers including Richard Condon and Frederick Forsyth tried it out for a few years, but most writers find that the temptations to do anything other than write, if you happen to be lucky enough to find yourself living in Ireland, are so strong that it is, on the whole, better to live anywhere else, get on with the work, and pay the taxes. It has, however, made life a whole lot easier for those Irish creative writers who have elected to stay on in Ireland.

So, too, did Haughey's second innovation, *Aosdana* (the word means poets, or wise men). This is a sort of 'academy' of about 150 creative Irish artists and writers, who are not required to do anything other than offer vague advice on various artistic matters, but who receive a 'fee' of about £6,000 a year, to eke out their meagre earnings from their chosen art or craft.

More recently, after the success of a number of Irish films like Roddy Doyle's *The Commitments* and the Oscar-winning *My Left Foot*, the Irish Government has started to offer tax breaks which effectively give film producers prepared to make their films on location in Ireland about ten to fifteen per cent of their budget back. The result of this has been an increase in investment in film production in Ireland from £1 million in 1992 to £100 million in 1994, and a proportion of this, of course, finds its way into the pockets and purses and tills of writers, actors, sound and lighting men as well as carpenters and caterers, not to mention all the supermarkets, stores, pubs, shops, hotels and restaurants lucky enough to find themselves near the chosen locations.

But although the poor Irish remain very poor, and the Irish middle-class, middle-income groups are among the most heavily-taxed in Europe, today's collection of Saint Patrick's people include a few individuals who have succeeded in achieving a very fancy life style indeed, among them the same Charlie Haughey; Tony O'Reilly, former international rugby star and director of the state-sponsored Milk Board; and top businessman Michael Smurfit.

Charles Haughey was an accountant by profession, though with the initial and very considerable added advantage of being married to the daughter of Sean Lemass, Premier of Ireland during the boom-time of the Swinging Sixties, and he managed to acquire, in the course of his career, a gracious Victorian mansion on forty-five acres in Raheny, just outside Dublin; a big farm in County Meath; a string of hunters and successful race horses; one of the Blasket Islands, Inishvicklane, off the coast of Kerry, on which he has built yet another mansion to which he travels back and forth either by luxury motor yacht or by helicopter; and the town house of Abbeyville, designed by James Gandon of Customs House fame for the Lords Lieutenant of Ireland, standing in 250 acres of prime land in County Dublin, as well as a vineyard in Burgundy.

Tony O'Reilly worked for an Bord Bainne (the Milk Board) marketing Irish butter world-wide under the brand-name Kerrygold. He then joined the Irish state-sponsored sugar monopoly, which also produced Erin freeze-dried foods. Next, he sold Erin foods to Heinz of the UK, then sold himself to Heinz as managing director

(UK) and wound up as Chief Executive of the company in Pittsburgh and the highest paid executive in the United States. He also controls the *Irish Independent* and a number of commercial radio stations in Ireland, and made a bid for the London *Daily Mirror* after the collapse of the Maxwell empire. He also has a stately mansion in Ireland, commutes across the Atlantic in a private jet and, like the hard Charlie, regularly uses a private helicopter to fulfil his social engagements.

Michael Smurfit inherited his (English) father's cardboard box factory in Dublin, expanded it into a worldwide container corporation paying over $1,200,000,000 for the Container Corporation of America. He now employs nearly 40,000 people, only 2,000 of whom live in Ireland. Like the others, he uses a helicopter on social occasions and is a big horse-race sponsor. He works from an office in Donnybrook, but is domiciled, for tax reasons, in Monte Carlo. His is not only Ireland's largest private company, but also the only one listed among the ten top companies in the world.

Saint Patrick would be altogether amazed at material success on such a scale.

7

Mother Church and Mary Robinson

Religion in Ireland

If Saint Patrick and the early bishops of the Christian Church in Ireland were extremely sympathetic to the views of their Celtic Irish converts, and were prepared to make considerable concessions to keep them within the fold, in spite of their defiantly deviant views on many matters including polygamy, the same could never be said of their successors. The portrait of the frustrated priest-confessor, dredging through the confused confessions of teenage courting couples for some hint of carnal gratification to be gloated over, before an appropriate penance was prescribed, is no figment of the imagination of Irish writers; and *The Dark* in which John McGahern's sad anti-hero played out his pathetic sexual fantasies is precisely the same kind of dark from the depths of which Ireland's celibate priests have for years pronounced on matters about which, in the nature of things, they could not possibly have any very deep or relevant understanding.

As comparatively recently as 1968, Donald S. Connery, a *Time-Life* London correspondent who spent a lot of his free time in Ireland in the late 1960s, wrote (in *The Irish*, London: Eyre and Spottiswode): 'Religion matters in Ireland more than in any other country in the English-speaking world.' It was so important, he claimed, that Irish atheists at that period fervently prayed to God that they might become believers, and he added that Northern Ireland, which is one-third Catholic, was the most passionately Protestant society he had ever encountered. In the five years he lived in London, he was only once asked his religion, and that was by an Irish priest who came to lunch one day.

Evidence that religion mattered more than anything else in Ireland, as well as that the Catholic Church throughout the English-speaking world was then very largely dominated by Irish clerics, was amply provided during the Eucharistic Congress of 1932, held to commemorate the 1,500th anniversary of Saint Patrick's arrival on Irish soil to start his ministry. The Irish Government, still struggling to repair the desperate damage done to the infrastructure during the troubled times, entertained 14,000 representatives of the Catholic Church from all over the world in great splendour at a mammoth garden party in the grounds of Blackrock College (Eamon de Valera's old school, and the school in which he taught mathematics in the period immediately before the Easter Rising of 1916) and over one million people attended an open-air mass in Phoenix Park. In the run-up to the Congress, according to Dermot Keogh (in *Twentieth Century Ireland: Nation and State*, Dublin: Gill & Macmillan, 1994), a total of 85,673,432 masses, benedictions and other acts of worship, piety and devotion were held. By the end of the Congress itself, that figure had reached the staggering total of 315,460,345, or 114 separate acts of worship or piety for every man, woman and child in the entire State.

That the Catholic Church in Ireland survived the Reformation was very largely due to the Irish language, a debt which the Catholic Church has never whole-heartedly acknowledged and has done little to repay.

At the time of the Reformation, the language of the overwhelming majority of Saint Patrick's successors was still Irish Gaelic, and no serious effort was ever made to convert the Catholic Irish to Protestantism because the bishops of the reformed church and the Tudor officials of the British Government did not speak a word of the only language through which that conversion might have been achieved. Though on reflection it seems unlikely that the Celts would have taken too kindly to any reformation of a religion which they felt they had inherited straight from Saint Patrick himself.

The Reformation was closely followed by the suppression of the monasteries, abbeys, convents and most of the other institutions which otherwise might have been used to assist the spread of the reformed religion. From the time of Henry VIII, the reformed Anglican Church was established as the Church of Ireland within the Pale – the area in Leinster and along the eastern seaboard where the British writ went largely unchallenged – but no great effort was made to extend its influence throughout the country as a whole, apart from the provision of parish churches for the convenience of the Protestant Anglo-Irish gentry, landlords and other settlers.

Indeed it was not until the defeat of the last British

Catholic king, James II, at the Battle of the Boyne in County Meath in 1690, and the consolidation of the Protestant succession in Britain by William of Orange and his wife, Mary (the Protestant daughter of James II), that the Catholic Church in Ireland was subjected to the pressure from which so much of its tenacious strength was subsequently derived. Incidentally, William of Orange, or King Billy, as he is known to his faithful followers in Ulster, derived his title from the old French town of Orange or *Arausio* in trans-Alpine Gaul, in Provençe, the first Roman external province. He in turn gave his name to the Orange Order, a semi-secret society run on similar lines to the Masonic Order, and founded in 1795 after a faction fight in Loughgall, County Antrim, to preserve the Protestant faith against all comers. Orange had become a separate principality at the time of Charlemagne and the title, Prince of Orange, was eventually passed on, by no less a person than the Holy Roman Emperor himself, to King Billy's family, the House of Nassau, which held scattered possessions in the Netherlands, Germany and France during the sixteenth century. Perhaps it's as well that not many Orangemen are aware of the papal connection.

For about a century after 1690, every effort was made to crush Catholicism and to destroy the Irish Catholics as a social class. Under the Penal Laws, the ordination of Catholic priests was prohibited, Catholic bishops were banished and Catholic religious orders were formally expelled. The punishment for priests and regular clergy who returned to their communities was death. On the other hand, Catholic priests who agreed to embrace the Protestant version of the faith were granted a state pension for life. All education was denied to Catholics,

Catholic schools became illegal and Catholic families were even forbidden to employ private tutors for their children, or to send them abroad to be educated. A reward of £10 was offered to anybody who informed on a Catholic teacher.

Perhaps even more importantly, as already mentioned, under these laws when a Catholic landowner died, his property was broken up among his sons instead of passing to the eldest son, although if one of the sons turned Protestant, he inherited all the land. By the middle of the eighteenth century, as a direct result of this legislation, combined with the policy of confiscating Irish lands after every rebellion and replanting them with loyal Protestants, less than ten per cent of all the land in Ireland remained in Catholic hands.

But aside from the effect they had upon the land-owning classes, the Penal Laws didn't really work in Ireland; a minority colony in an alien country could never employ enough spies and policemen, official or unofficial, to ensure that all the regulations were being observed. And in practice, the Penal Laws often had precisely the opposite effect from that which had been originally intended. Many Catholics, educated in the first instance in hedge schools (unofficial Catholic classes, run by priests and often held in the open air, hence the title), which immediately sprang up as soon as the Catholic schools were closed down, escaped to the European mainland, where they continued their education and were eventually ordained as priests. They then returned to minister to the people, living on the run and sharing the lives of the peasants, celebrating mass in caves, or in clearings in the woods, as well as secretly in the homes of Catholic families.

These unusual arrangements drew the priests and their congregations into a far closer intimacy than ever could have been achieved under the formal parochial framework, and greatly strengthened both the Irish devotion to their priests and the hold of the priests over their flocks. And, since other Penal Laws now made it impossible for Catholics to occupy positions of any importance in the army or in the public services, or to become lawyers or Members of Parliament, most of the best brains among the Catholic Irish tended to emigrate, leaving the priests as the sole and unchallenged leaders of thought in Ireland.

What is slightly more difficult to understand is how the priests managed to retain that influence in the years that followed. Towards the end of the eighteenth century, the British tried out a very different policy. By adopting a conciliatory attitude towards the Catholics in Ireland, Pitt tried to achieve some measure of control over the Irish Catholic Church. The first step he took was to found, in 1795, at Maynooth in County Kildare, a seminary for the training of Irish priests, and it was no coincidence that St Patrick's College was initially staffed largely by pro-monarchy refugees fleeing from the French Revolution. It was greatly in Britain's interest that Irish priests should be taught their trade by these conservative and law-abiding theologians, rather than that they should learn it in post-revolutionary, anti-monarchist France. To some extent at least, Rome connived in this policy, possibly in the hope that a loyal Catholic Ireland within the framework of the United Kingdom could be used as a base from which to continue to exert some pressure on Britain, or possibly merely in the hope of getting a solid bloc of influential Catholics into the Parliament at Westminster, after the Union.

In 1803, in an effort to secure a firmer grip on the Catholic Church in Ireland, Pitt proposed to allow Catholic Emancipation on condition that the British Government would be allowed to veto any bishop of whom it disapproved. Initially, Rome was also prepared to go along with this compromise, but Daniel O'Connell, an Irish politician who was just then beginning to weld the Catholic Irish into some semblance of a nation, would have none of it. Rome for faith, but not for politics, was one of his mottoes, and in the end, by attending the Parliament at Westminster on 4 February, 1830, in open defiance of King George IV, he won full Catholic Emancipation, including the right of Catholics to sit at Westminster.

Once the Catholic Church had been accepted by the authorities, the Catholic hierarchy opposed almost all of the Irish nationalist and revolutionary movements. And although during the Land War the local parish priest was often the focus of agitation against unjust landlords, it was usually against the express wishes of his bishop. It was an Irish Catholic bishop (Bishop David Moriarty of the Diocese of Kerry) who declared that hell was not hot enough, nor eternity long enough, to punish the Fenian leaders. Some at least of the Irish Catholic bishops were strongly opposed to the 1916 Rising, although the hierarchy did not condemn it. The bishops were, however, so bitterly opposed to the stand made by the anti-Treaty Irregulars in 1922 that they excommunicated, for a time, some of the men who were later to lead the Irish State, and many of the Irregulars died without the consolation of the sacraments.

That the priests did not lose their hold over the Irish

people during the period leading up to the Troubles and during the War of Independence and the Civil War was due to a number of factors. First, only a minority of the Irish people were in favour, at the start, of a complete break with England. The farmers had been doing extremely well as a result of the new British policy of appeasement and would readily have agreed with the bishops that nothing much was to be gained by armed resistance.

Then, the success of the Land War, which had the effect of removing the landlords and turning the Irish tenant farmers into a race of peasant proprietors, had left a vacuum in the rural communities which came to be dominated more and more by the priests because there was no other élite in a community of more or less equally poor and certainly equally unadventurous small farmers from which it could be filled. The British had already effectively put the priests in charge of education in Ireland by appointing them managers of the new Catholic national schools that they were providing as part of their policy of appeasement. And in the absence of any other aristocracy, it was natural that the Irish would tend to turn to their priests for advice, not merely on religious and educational matters, but on secular issues such as agricultural co-operation, legal squabbles and even on such mundane matters as the granting of licences for pubs and dance halls.

And, whatever about the hierarchy, many of the local parish priests managed to retain the close ties with the people which had existed since the early days of the Penal Laws. Some of them turned a blind eye to the instructions of their bishops – even to the extent of administering the last rites to dying Irregulars – and while not many of them took a very progressive nationalistic line, at least they spoke in a voice that was recognisably more Irish than that of the Anglican Church of Ireland, which was clearly identified in the Irish mind with English oppression.

Although most of the uprisings and rebellions against British rule had been masterminded by Protestants, the Sinn Fein movement which in the end achieved a limited measure of freedom for twenty-six of the thirty-two Irish counties in 1921 was almost entirely a Catholic outfit, and the pro-Treaty party which ran the Irish Free State for the first decade or so of its existence was abjectly subservient in pandering to all the suspicions and susceptibilities of the hierarchy.

And although it was equally true that women – among others, Maud Gonne, Countess Markievicz and Lady Gregory – had been in the forefront of all the movements that led to Irish freedom, it wasn't until the 1970s that an Irish government appointed a female minister.

And it was unfortunate that Maynooth, during the period immediately before and after the Rising, had fallen into the grip of a particularly joyless, puritanical ethic, imported from France along with the Jansenist priests brought over to run the seminary. And equally unfortunate that the ordinary people in Dublin and indeed throughout Ireland had, at the same time, succumbed to an extremely prissy set of Victorian English views on morals and manners.

A combination of all these factors, on top of the general feeling of isolation which had resulted from the confusion caused by the War of Independence and the Civil War, led to a certain amount of repressive legislation of which the Censorship of Publications Act was the one which attracted most international attention, though other matters, such as the lack of any provision for divorce, the total ban on contraception, and the ban imposed by successive Catholic Archbishops of Dublin forbidding Catholics to attend Trinity College, probably did far more real damage. The intellectuals who wanted to read the banned books could very easily get their hands on copies and most of the ordinary Irish people wouldn't have read them anyway, though the fact that the Irish Censorship Board banned most of the books (including many by leading Irish writers) which would have been on any list of required reading for a degree in literature, made the new State look pretty silly in the eyes of the world.

Films were another matter, though, because ever since the days of the Keystone Cops and Felix the Cat, the Irish have been compulsive cinema-goers. Indeed, very early on in the history of the motion picture industry, they acquired a devotion to the moving image every bit as deep as their devotion to the holy statues and lurid depictions of the Sacred Heart which used to constitute the only works of art, if you could call them that, to be found in most of their homes.

The Irish passion for moving pictures reached its full flowering with the advent of television. But, whereas it had been easy enough, in the early days of the State, to ensure that an industrious film censor would screen every foot of celluloid imported into the country, and remove every inch of film likely in any way to undermine the innate, natural chastity and innocence of the Irish race, as conceived by those early governments of the State, television, it was soon discovered, could not so easily be censored.

An article in the literary review *Envoy* in the 1950s

suggested that the government ministers of the period were considering the possibilities of an interceptor-transmitter, sited perhaps on the summit of Howth Head, which could be used to scramble 'undesirable' images. But if they ever did consider such a scheme, it didn't come to anything, and a diet of thirty-odd years of undiluted British television has resulted in a situation in which the children of the chaste Christian innocents of the mid-twentieth century have by now far outstripped the rest of the world's offspring in a degree of permissiveness that verges on encouragement of, if not actual exhortation to, what used to be regarded as the very gravest sort of sins. This revolution has been coupled with a total rejection of all accepted values, which reached its absurd zenith (or perhaps nadir might be a more appropriate word) in Ireland's Madonna, the singer Sinead O'Connor, who not only shaved all the hair off her head and appeared in public with a pate as bald as Yul Brynner's, but also publicly tore up a picture of the Pope during the course of an American coast-to-coast television chat show.

Up to about a decade ago, homosexuality was still an unspeakable offence for which Irishmen could be sent to prison; not only is homosexuality between consenting adults no longer against the law, but by 1994, newspapers were carrying advertisements for a Gay and Lesbian (though there's really no need for the lesbians to shout so loudly about it, because lesbianism was never against the law, much as they may bitterly regret that fact) Film Festival in Cork, and were listing a selection of forthcoming Irish publications including works entitled *Coming Out: A Book for Lesbians and Gay Men of All Ages*, *Quare Fellas*, a new anthology of writing by gay men and *Sugar and Spice: A Lesbian Anthology*.

And, while as relatively recently as thirty years ago unmarried mothers, as they were then known, were treated as outcasts, one-parent families, as they are now called, are as common in Ireland as they are elsewhere, and are treated with the same courtesy and respect as families with the traditional quota of parents.

Perhaps the really surprising thing is not that today's young successors to the Celtic tradition are so coruscatingly liberated, but that their parents and grandparents mindlessly allowed themselves to be moulded by Church and State into such a dismal collection of narrow-minded, nervous, conventional conformists, terrified by sex, scared stiff of their priests and a very far cry indeed from their feisty forebears.

In *Ireland Since the Rising* (London: Pall Mall, 1966) Tim Pat Coogan wrote: 'An undue hostility to foreign influences (mainly to things English) and a concentration on the pastoral aspects of Irish culture have tended to create an uneasy vision in the public mind of what the country would be like if the Gaels ever controlled it.' By the Gaels he meant the new language fanatics who insisted that everything should be learned and taught 'through the medium' of the Irish language.

'The concept of the Gael as propagated by the extreme wing of the movement,' he went on, 'is of a man approximately six feet and five inches in height, noble-browed and with the faraway look in his eyes which comes through perusing Erin's past glories. His wife is serene, beautiful and the mother of eleven children. In view of the mandatory chastity of the couple, conception, it will be understood, occurs non-sexually – through the medium, as it were.'

De Valera certainly contributed to this concept with

his own austere vision of the Irish Dream: a land of innocent lads and chaste lasses, dancing the jig at the crossroads, with no stronger stimulant in sight than a glass of buttermilk. In a radio broadcast to the nation, on Saint Patrick's Day, 17 March 1943, he said: 'The Ireland which we have dreamed of would be the home of a people who valued material wealth only as the basis of a right living, of a people who were satisfied with frugal comfort and devoted their leisure to the things of the spirit; a land whose countryside would be bright with cosy homesteads, whose fields and villages would be joyous with the sounds of industry, with the romping of sturdy children, the contests of athletic youths, the laughter of comely maidens; a place whose firesides would be forums for the wisdom of old age.'

Tabloid English newspapers, evil literature, 'suggestive' magazines, mixed bathing and, above all, 'jazz-dancing', also known as 'foreign' or 'imported' dancing, were all castigated from the pulpits as outward and visible signs of the corruption of the age, and even company-keeping, that most rudimentary form of courtship, was frowned upon by Mother Church.

Dermot Keogh, author of the book, *Twentieth Century Ireland*, mentioned above, quotes Archbishop Gilmartin of Tuam, admonishing his flock in December 1926: 'Company keeping under the stars of night has succeeded in too many places the good old Irish custom of visiting, chatting and story-telling from one house to another, with the Rosary to bring all home in due time.'

When I was growing up in Dublin, a heavy petting session was known as a 'hot court' (pronounced coort), and intercourse, which was discussed among the young bloods far more often than it was ever practised, was known – perhaps in deference to Ireland's long association with the horse industry – as 'gettin' a ride'.

By the 1950s the same activity was known as 'doing the bold thing', and even well into the 1960s offences like buggery and rape were always referred to in the newspapers simply as 'serious offences'. Now four-letter words, including the formerly dreaded f– word, are sprinkled almost as liberally through the Irish newspapers as they are throughout Roddy Doyle's novels, and young, liberated female columnists write about bonking as if it were as natural and unremarkable a human activity as eating or washing the dishes, which I daresay it is to them and their generation, and why not?

From a recent column in the *Irish Times*, I also gather that the current state-of-the-art parental guidelines on bringing up children recommend that if your son invites his girlfriend to stay with him overnight, it is perfectly okay for you to accept that they are sleeping together, but it is not okay to accord your daughter the same privilege, unless, of course, she has elected to stay overnight at her boyfriend's home, in which case his parents will provide the parental *imprimatur* over breakfast the next morning. This *imprimatur* is, of course, a matter of concern only to the parents involved; the article made it perfectly clear that the young people have no feelings on the subject themselves, nor do they care in the slightest what their parents feel about it.

It would be tedious as well as unnecessary to try to trace all the steps that have contributed, inch by painful inch, to the dramatic change in the Irish attitude towards sex and the decline in the influence of Mother Church which has taken place since the 1920s, but it might be useful to glance at a few of the major milestones along the way.

For the first few decades before and after the formation of the new Irish State, as a result of some whim on the part of nature, or of natural selection perhaps, far more girls were born than boys, and as it was always far easier for boys to emigrate, a girl born in Ireland at any time between 1845 and 1945 had less chance of getting married than a girl from any other country in the world.

The girls' problems in this respect were further compounded by the fact that very few of the young men who left home and remained in Ireland could ever afford to marry: there were no jobs for them. The eldest son, who normally stayed on in the farm in the hope of inheriting it when his parents eventually died, was usually far too old when that finally happened to be much interested in, or of much interest to, any bride he might then acquire, and he probably greatly preferred to spend his evenings chatting and drinking porter in the pub anyway, thus also avoiding the occasion of sin. As Donald Connery remarked in his book, *The Irish*, until the late 1960s Ireland was still a country where marriage was regarded as a licence to sin. Sexual intercourse, even within the borders of the marriage bed, as O'Casey put it, was still regarded as a grave sin.

'Well-known for its bachelors and spinsters,' he went on, 'it is perhaps the one place in the world where men most effectively manage to continue their bachelor pursuits (which have little to do with sex) after marriage. It has the greatest percentage of virgins, the fewest divorces [since divorce was then forbidden] and the least emancipated women in the English-speaking world.'

Some statistics: in 1930, the proportion of unmarried males in the under-thirty age-group was eighty per cent, and the total of unmarried females in the twenty-five to thirty-year-old age group was sixty-two per cent, as against forty-one per cent in the United Kingdom and twenty-three per cent in the United States. But other statistics seem to indicate that not all of the Irish men elected to spend all their evenings in the pub. The early governments of the new State were constantly worried about the unprecedented increase in the rate of illegitimate births after independence, and perturbed by the number of places in the county homes being taken up by unmarried mothers and their babies, greatly to the embarrassment of the – so to speak – legitimate inmates of these charitable institutions, the deserving poor. Come to think of it, illegitimate is an odd word anyway, because it is not against any law to have a baby out of wedlock.

Convinced that 'evil literature' emanating from the godless kingdom across the water was, aside from jazz dancing, another of the contributory causes of these lapses from grace by innocent and gullible Irish maidens, the government rushed through a bill setting up a Censorship Board of five Irish citizens to consider any book about which any complaint was made to them, and to ban books and magazines by the dozen or by the gross, either because they appeared to be, in their view, 'in general tendency indecent and obscene', or because they contained any reference whatsoever, for or against, to the forbidden topic of birth control. Initially, it had been planned that the board would consist of a representative of the Catholic Church, a doctor, a lawyer and one representative each from Trinity College, Dublin, and from the National University of Ireland. As time went by, however, and since the members of the Censorship Board were unpaid, it became increasingly difficult to find anybody to serve on the board and its membership varied greatly.

Some notion of the naïve, puritanical atmosphere in which the Board was conceived can be gleaned by glancing through the reports of the debates on the subject in the Dail and Senate. The then Minister for Justice, Fitzgerald Kenney, remarked in the course of one of the discussions that although Becky Sharp was obviously an immoral woman, nobody could properly condemn *Vanity Fair*. The suggestion clearly was that he would feel far happier if the Irish could be restricted to reading books about moral women, and, after speculating on Othello's morals, he added, as a rule of thumb, that the Board 'must not, because it has a great name behind it, be terrified into not condemning a book which should be condemned.'

Another representative of the Irish electorate gave it as his considered opinion that James Joyce's *Ulysses* was not the sort of book anybody would need to read before deciding to ban it, though, curiously enough, it has never been banned in Ireland. And during a debate on divorce around the same time, Professor William Magennis summed up the Catholic attitude to the entire situation by concluding: 'You cannot be a good Catholic if you allow divorce, even among Protestants.'

In the 1950s, the big scandal was the unanimous rejection by the hierarchy of Noel Browne's 'Mother-and-Child' scheme. It was the first attempt by a young and radical health minister, Dr Noel Browne, to introduce a tiny measure of social welfare – a measure of ante- and post-natal care free, without a means test, for mothers and children – and it was immediately and bitterly opposed by the hierarchy on the grounds that it was the responsibility of the father of the family to provide for, or, if it so happens, to fail utterly to provide for, the health of his wife and children, and that any attempt on the part of the State to intervene amounted to a form of socialist fascism.

'The State has the right to intervene only in a subsidiary capacity,' the hierarchy argued, 'to supplement, not to supplant. It may help indigent or neglectful parents, [but] it may not deprive 90 per cent of the parents of their rights because of 10 per cent necessitous or negligent parents.' Within a few years, after Noel Browne had been sacked and the Inter-Party Coalition Government which deserted him at the first flash of the crozier had disappeared into limbo, a far more comprehensive welfare scheme was introduced by a later government and accepted by the hierarchy without a peep, because they realised that times had changed.

In the 1960s, the contraceptive pill arrived on the scene. Because it was a pill, and not some sort of a mechanical device, such as a condom or a diaphragm, Irish women proved readier to accept it, and their doctors readier to prescribe it, though always for the purpose of regularising their patients' periods, so that they could use the so-called 'safe' period, as prescribed by Mother Church. The fact that once they were on the pill, the Irish women didn't need to use the safe period, or any other system of contraception, was neither here nor there, either to them or their doctors.

The special position of the Catholic Church as being the religion of the majority of the Irish people, which had been expressly guaranteed by de Valera's 1937 Constitution, was quietly dropped in 1972 after a half-hearted referendum, and in the same year the Archbishop of Dublin decided that it was no longer a sin for Catholics to attend Trinity College.

A projected bill to make contraceptives easier to come by, proposed by a Labour Senator, Mary Robinson, in the 1970s, fell by the wayside, but when a Mrs Mary McGee took a specific case to the Supreme Court in December 1973, it was ruled that it was not unconstitutional to import contraceptives for personal use. Legislation was hurriedly introduced to make the sale of contraceptives legal, though initially only to married people of eighteen years of age and older. A Catholic priest later gave it as his considered opinion that, despite the Pope's condemnation of the use of contraceptives in any circumstances, they could be justified in the case of married people, and provided that they were only being used as a protection against Aids, and not for the purpose of avoiding conception. This was a very good example of a curious form of double-think which less charitable observers of the Irish scene might classify as hypocrisy of a very determined nature.

A marriage bill, first circulated in July 1972, raised the marriage age to sixteen; it had previously been fourteen for boys and twelve for girls in Ireland. By 1979 government ministers were less concerned by the number of illegitimate births in the Republic than by the 'Abortion Trail', as it was called: the number of Irish women who were going to England to have abortions. There seems to be general agreement that the figure averaged around 4,000 a year during the 1980s and early 1990s.

In 1966 the hierarchy decided to accord mixed marriages the same blessings from the Church as had previously been reserved for Catholics prepared to promise that their children would be brought up in the faith. In the same year, the seminary at Maynooth decided to open its doors to nuns and lay pupils of both sexes as well as prospective priests; it has since become a coeducational university with as many female students as male ones, and far more, certainly, than the total of prospective priests.

By 1995 only the aggravating issues of divorce and abortion remained to be solved, the pair of them always lumped together in Dublin parlance, as the 'distortion' issue. During the course of two terms in office as Taoiseach, Garret Fitzgerald, whose mother was a Presbyterian from the North of Ireland, had tried to argue the case for pluralism in such matters as a prerequisite for any closer rapprochement between the six severed counties of Northern Ireland and the Irish State. The divorce issue was finally settled when a referendum in November 1995 decided to drop the specific ban on divorce from the constitution – but only by a whisker, 9,000 votes or less than half of one per cent of the electorate.

The issue of abortion cropped up in the early 1980s after a United States Supreme Court judgment declared the American anti-abortion legislation to be unconstitutional. Fitzgerald, believing that the majority of Irish people, north and south alike, were instinctively opposed to the whole notion of abortion, tried to find a formula for an amendment to the Irish Constitution which would rule out any repetition of what had happened in America. But he did not find it easy, and was in opposition when the subject resurfaced in 1982. The government party of that period, led by Charles Haughey, came up with an amendment which caused an outcry from doctors, lawyers and interested laymen who argued that the amendment was ambiguous on the question of whose life was to be protected and which left it open to the courts to outlaw operations to save the life of the mother, until then routinely carried out in all Irish hospitals.

In 1983, Fitzgerald, back in power, appealed to the hierarchy, which supported the Haughey amendment, stating that it would 'greatly contribute to the continued protection of human life [that of the unborn child, as well as that of the mother] in the laws of our country', and that seemed good enough for the electorate, who voted two to one in favour of the amendment in a referendum in September 1983.

Mary Robinson, a very successful barrister and former Labour Senator, had resigned from the party in protest against the Coalition Government's failure to consult the Ulster Unionists in advance over the All Ireland Forum, an attempt by Garret Fitzgerald to embody the views of all parties in Ireland, north and south, about partition and the future of Northern Ireland. In 1989, she appeared for the defence in a case against four students from Trinity College, Dublin, who had distributed information about where abortions could be obtained. An anti-abortion society known as SPUC (the Society for the Protection of the Unborn Child) had won an injunction to prevent the Trinity students from disseminating any advice on abortion, and when four of them continued to distribute their leaflets regardless, they were charged with contempt of court. Mary Robinson argued that the real question at issue was whether any group of people in any one European Community state, attempting to advertise a service which was freely available in another European Community state, could legitimately be prevented from doing so by any pressure group. She argued that the nature of the service which was on offer (in this case, abortion) was irrelevant, and that the whole matter was one for the European Court of Justice at Luxembourg to decide.

The judge in the case, who also happened to be a woman,

Mrs Justice Mella Carroll, referred the whole matter to the European Court and warned SPUC that a ruling might not come for a year or more and that, in the meantime, no action could be taken against the Trinity students. The latter, wearing shirts emblazoned with the legend 'SPUC YOU', celebrated in the streets of Dublin and continued to peddle information about facilities for abortion to Trinity freshmen, or, more accurately, freshwomen.

Within two years, Mary Robinson, a feminist with extremely radical views on many subjects aside from the 'Distortion Issue', and married to a Protestant into the bargain, was elected President of Ireland, with a majority of 86,000.

Then in the early 1990s, the abortion issue again reared its ugly head. Albert Reynolds's coalition government collapsed in November 1994, when his deputy Dick Spring, the Labour leader, discovered that Reynolds had promoted Attorney-General Harry Whelehan to the post of Head of the High Court without even consulting his partners in government. Albert Reynolds's enemies took that as an attempt to put Whelehan in a position in which he could not be legally questioned about the fact that as Attorney-General, he, or some of his senior civil servants, had appeared to obstruct, for several months, an extradition order for a Northern Ireland priest who had been a known paederast for years. It then emerged that the Catholic Church had been fully aware of the priest's proclivities, and had been constantly moving him from post to post within the Republic to keep him out of harm's way, so to speak. And matters were not improved by the fact that this was the same Attorney-General who had precipitated events in the notorious 'Miss X' case by referring the matter to the Director of Public Prosecutions, who instructed the police to have 'Miss X', as she was known in court, brought back to Ireland.

'Miss X', it will be remembered, was a fourteen-year-old girl who had been raped and made pregnant by a neighbour old enough to be her father, and had been taken to England by her parents to have an abortion. When her parents contacted the police to ensure that if any DNA tests should be taken, they would be acceptable as evidence in any court proceedings which might follow, the police referred the matter to 'higher authority' and the Department of Public Prosecutions ordered that the girl be returned to Dublin and prevented from leaving Ireland again, to have an abortion. It was only after an appeal to the Supreme Court that a decision was made that it was unconstitutional to stop a young woman (who had suicidal tendencies and was as much entitled to the 'right to life', as specified in the amendment to the 1937 Constitution, as the unborn foetus), from travelling to England for the purpose of having an abortion, that the matter was, in part at least, cleared up. The affair ended with a referendum in which the public voted overwhelmingly for an amendment to the Constitution giving pregnant women the right to acquire information about abortion and to travel abroad for the purpose of obtaining one, though a second amendment designed to clear up the very tricky 'right to life' aspect of the matter was defeated, and has not yet been finally resolved. Fresh legislation on the subject is currently (March 1995) under discussion in the course of a Supreme Court hearing of an appeal challenging as unconstitutional the act allowing information on abortion to be disseminated, which had been hurriedly rushed through Parliament after the referendum.

Alongside this glimpse of Catholic confusion, the

peccadilloes of the bold Bishop Casey seem trivial. All he did, after all, was to take the daughter of a relative who had had an unhappy marriage in America into his home to offer her some counselling, in the course of which he happened to make her pregnant. At least they were both heterosexual and Ms Annie Murphy was old enough to give her consent to His Grace's advances, which she clearly did. There was, of course, also the fact that he admitted diverting over £70,000 from diocesan funds for his son's upkeep and, presumably, to ensure Ms Murphy's continuing silence on the matter. The sum in the event proved inadequate, and in 1992 Ms Murphy revealed all, again and again, in a book, in newspaper interviews, and on television chat shows all over the place.

The more recent revelations that at least a dozen Catholic priests were under investigation, both north and south of the border, for child abuse, angered the Irish people who felt that they had been hoodwinked, over the years, by the clergy, and for the first time in Irish history, priests now run the risk of being ridiculed in the streets.

Some of the credit for this new liberation must go, I think, to Gay Byrne whose very popular open-ended talkathon *The Late, Late Show* has consistently, over the past thirty years, remained about ten years ahead of its time in its attitude towards controversial issues. As well as some light-hearted *News of the World* type revelations – a famous one was a show away back in the 1950s during which he asked a number of respectable, middle-aged Irish housewives what they had worn in bed on their wedding night, and on a more recent occasion when interviewing Ms Annie Murphy, he told her that he only hoped her son would grow up to be half the man his father was – he has frequently dealt very seriously and openly with topics never previously discussed on the air on a popular television programme. And some of the most outspoken and radical views were those expressed by a new generation of young priests.

Young is the key word here and, perhaps in the last analysis, what has happened in Ireland is not only that there has been what has been described as a youth explosion – nearly fifty per cent of the population is now under twenty-five years of age – but also that the young people are challenging many of the old beliefs and prejudices and, for the first time, are being listened to, even by senior politicians, in a way that would have been unthinkable, even a generation ago.

The Church is losing some of its authority, certainly. To what extent it is difficult to say. Official statistics put today's Catholic population in Ireland at ninety-five per cent, and reckon that the average attendances at mass every Sunday work out at around eighty to eighty-five per cent. If this is true, which I find hard to believe, it may be because of social pressures: a natural reluctance to offend parents, a deep dislike of giving the neighbours something else to complain about, a state of sheer apathy, perhaps, in which it seems far easier to go along with what your parents want than to strike out against them for no good reason, carrying more weight perhaps than personal conviction. I don't believe for a moment that it has much to do with religion; almost all of the Irish emigrants in London and New York I have interviewed told me that they stopped going to mass as soon as they left Ireland.

The figures may look good in the statistics, but if I were the Pope, I wouldn't count on the continuing, unquestioning fidelity of the new generation of Saint Patrick's people.

8

Through the Medium

The Irish Language

When Saint Patrick began his conversion of the Irish Celts, the language they spoke was Irish Gaelic, one of a group of Celtic languages still spoken in Cornwall, in parts of Wales and Scotland and in what is now Brittany in France, so called because it was a colony set up by Celts from Britain. The forms of the language spoken in these places are very different from Irish Gaelic but, then again, several dialects of Irish Gaelic were spoken in Ireland, and Irish-speakers from County Donegal probably experienced about the same level of difficulty in understanding fellow Irish-speakers from County Kerry, as English-speaking people from the Home Counties now have in understanding the dialect used by Geordies from Tyneside.

The ancient Irish language – the earliest Celtic language which can be reconstructed from written sources anywhere – was picked up initially by Saint Patrick's Breton followers and their successors who, through the medium of Latin, codified it and turned it into a written language with a formal syntax. At the same time they taught the illiterate Celts how to read and write, not only in Latin but also in their own language, a fairly formidable achievement when you come to think about it.

The Irish language has been a recognised subject for serious study at Trinity College, Dublin, ever since the university was founded in 1591 and primarily perhaps, as Maire Cruise O'Brien remarks in her contribution, 'The Two Languages', in *Ireland*, edited by Owen Dudley Edwards (London: André Deutsch, 1969), 'because of its utility in converting the heathen, but also, one must believe, a little bit for its own sake and a love, however suppressed, of things Irish generally'.

Irish remained the everyday language of Saint Patrick's people right up to the time of the Great Famine, and was also cultivated and adopted by many of the Anglo-Irish. To quote Maire Cruise O'Brien again: 'The Protestant community in Ireland had no other home. Settled for centuries in most cases, augmented by native stock, they were bound to the Irish scene by all the normal human pieties as well as by the interests of a dominant class ... Rejected as being Irish by the English, the more passionate and stormy spirits among them tended to become even more strongly what they were in fact already, in all but formal loyalties, Irish.'

But the million or so deaths during the Great Famine, and the mass emigration which followed it, robbed the country of a very high proportion of its native Irish speakers until by the end of the Second World War, only about 55,000 people, or approximately two per cent of the population, spoke Irish as their first language. These were people who lived in areas in the west and south-west of Ireland known collectively as the Gaeltacht. Since

1946, no real effort has been made to discover, through the census papers, how many people still speak Irish Gaelic (the question is now so vaguely phrased that anybody who knows what *Cead Mile Failte* means can claim to be an Irish speaker), though the Dublin Institute of Advanced Studies reckoned in 1951 that 'no more than 35,000 people now use Irish as their ordinary medium of speech, and no more than 3,000 are ignorant of English'.

Since then, as Terence Brown remarks in *Ireland: A Social and Cultural History, 1922–1979* (London: Fontana, 1989): 'The economic revival in the west of the country in the 1970s reflected, for example, in the rapid rise in the population of Galway, has it seems, reinforced the tendency of Gaelic-speaking and partly Gaelic-speaking districts to abandon the Irish language altogether for English, the language of tourism and of the multinational corporations and foreign companies that have located factories west of the Shannon in the last twenty years.'

The Irish freedom-fighters of the War of Independence fought for an Ireland that would not only be free but would also be Irish-speaking. De Valera once said that if he had to choose between an Ireland that was Irish-speaking and an Ireland that was free, he would unhesitatingly choose the former. This may sound like extravagant nonsense, but what he probably meant was that if only the language could be saved before it was too late, the fight for freedom could be taken up at any time; on the other hand, if the language were allowed to die, it could never be revived, and an essential element in the Irish character would be lost for ever.

While I was writing an earlier book about Ireland, an Englishman asked me what use was Irish. The answer, if you look at it from a purely practical point of view, must be no use at all. There is no practical justification whatever for trying to keep a dead language alive. That same Englishman, however, happened to be a prominent member of the World Wide Fund for Nature and spent a lot of his time and energy raising funds for the preservation of the rhinoceros and the African elephant and various other species of wild animals in grave danger of becoming extinct. What use is a rhinoceros? From the practical point of view, about as much use as the Irish language. But, as I wrote at the time, 'the rhinoceros and the Irish language are both relics of the splendid diversity that life used to offer before we all became engulfed in this terrible tidal wave of cement and plastic and Coca Cola prosperity, and the world would be a poorer place if either of them was allowed to disappear.'

The earliest governments of the new Irish Free State were determined to make the State Irish-speaking, and right from the outset tried to re-establish Irish as the principal language of the country, even to the extent of insisting that all school books in Irish be printed in Gaelic script, a measure which cost an inordinate amount of money because special fonts had to be manufactured to print them. This Gaelic script was in any case based on a rather fancy type-face designed for the first edition of the New Testament in Irish in the time of Elizabeth I; in any event, a perfectly workable system of reproducing what Saint Patrick's disciples had salvaged of the old Irish language had been evolved using Roman characters, and was used for printing all state papers, which were initially printed both in Irish and English.

De Valera's new Constitution of 1939, composed, it was said at the time, in collaboration with John Charles

McQuaid, the Catholic Archbishop of Dublin, not only acknowledged God as the ultimate Head of State and recognised the 'special position' of the Catholic Church as the religion of the majority of the people, as well as claiming territorial rights over those parts of Ireland not at that time, or at any time since, under Irish jurisdiction, but also stipulated Irish as the national language and the first official language of the State and merely 'recognised' English as a second official language.

The early governments of the Irish Free State uprooted all the British road signs and replaced them with signposts in Irish only. New green and white name-plates appeared on the walls in towns and cities, giving all the street names in Irish on top, and underneath – to ensure that people would continue to get their mail – in English. Of the other signs which began to appear in Irish only, *Telefon and Bus* presented no problems but to decide, when faced with a public lavatory labelled only in Gaelic, as many of them were well into the 1960s, whether *Fir* or *Mna* looked the better bet, must have presented an agonising problem for many a hard-pressed foreign visitor.

As long ago as 1948, the Government switched to English only for all official forms and most correspondence, except in the Gaeltacht areas, and many of the all-Irish signposts were in turn uprooted and replaced by the familiar international signs. These days motorists approaching road works are no longer puzzled by the strange phrase *Fir Ag Obair*, which means 'Men at Work', but was often taken by tourists who had grown accustomed to the *Fir* and *Mna* business, as indicating the proximity of a gents' lavatory. This sign has now been replaced by the standard symbolic silhouette of a workman, bent over his industrious spade.

The early governments of the State made the Irish language compulsory in all schools and a qualifying subject for the Intermediate and Leaving schools certificates – roughly equivalent to the old English O and A levels – as well as for admittance into, or advancement within, the civil service.

Perhaps it was that word 'compulsory' which did so much damage to these early efforts to revive or rescue the language. And yet for schoolchildren, all lessons are compulsory; if they weren't, few children would learn anything from choice. And the policy of compulsory Irish did keep the language alive, at least to an extent. Without it, the language would already be as dead as the dodo. As it is, a great many Irish people now in what the French with their discerning delicacy have christened the third age, know a lot more Irish than they think they do; they couldn't hold an intelligent conversation in the language, perhaps, but they have a sufficient smattering of it to catch the drift of a radio bulletin in Irish. And that is a lot better than nothing.

In my anatomy of Ireland, *The Irish Answer* (London: Heinemann, 1966) I wrote: 'The attempt to encourage schoolmasters to teach other subjects, such as history and geography, through the medium of Irish, was not as crazy either as we used to think it was. If it had worked, it would have given us a fluency in Irish which we could never have achieved merely by learning the language as a separate subject in itself. Nor is the argument that it would have been better to concentrate all the effort wasted on Irish upon French or German or some other living European language entirely valid; because all the evidence of modern research into language teaching tends to indicate that once you break down the monolingual barrier – once students get into the frame of mind in which they realise that a thought can be expressed in more than one form of words – it becomes easier, and not more difficult, to learn a third or a fourth language.'

This argument seems to have been validated by the emergence in recent years – long after the state-imposed efforts to have other subjects taught through the medium had been dropped in despair – of a number of new schools that do all their main teaching in Irish, with English hardly used at all. 'This is not a scheme imposed by the Government, as in the 1920s,' writes John Ardagh in *Ireland and the Irish*, 'it came first from local parent demand, and then received state funding. Schools of this kind had been dwindling away, except in the rural Gaeltacht areas, but since 1972 the total of Irish-language primary schools has risen from 11 to 80, while that of secondary schools has risen from 8 to 20, nearly all of them in urban areas.'

I had almost completed this book when John Ardagh's very fully-researched study of the changing Irish was published but I was gratified to discover that most of his findings and conclusions paralleled mine. And, almost echoing my remarks above, made in 1965, about preserving Irish as a bulwark against the tidal wave of cement and plastic and Coca Cola prosperity that threatens to engulf us all, he quotes a middle-class parent of children attending one of these new Irish-language schools as saying: 'We are not ourselves Irish-speakers, but Ireland's language is a defence against its being swamped by Anglo-American culture, that's why we send our children to one of these schools.' That's why, too, it has recently become 'chic', as he puts it, to speak Irish, and he talks of

Irish couples abroad who converse in Irish in public places in order to ensure that they will not be mistaken for English.

And this new attitude to the language, and particularly to the ancient culture, is reflected in the names the young Irish people are choosing for their children. Even the staid columns of the *Irish Times*, which in my time used to record the ongoing procession of Georges and Johns and Gertrudes and Margarets, now list dynasties of Killians, Aislings, Fergals, Oisins, Nialls and Caoiltes. You might also be inclined to draw the conclusion from the number of births announced in the Brendan and Aoife format (i.e., Brendan and Aoife are thrilled by the happy birth of their beautiful son Cuchulain Caoilte who came out to play on 23 August 1994) that this indicates a big increase in Ireland in the number of people who have decided to increase and multiply without the benefit of the Church's blessing. It might be so, but not necessarily; it could be merely that this is the way young people choose to announce the arrival of their offspring these days.

The initial attempt to make the new State Irish-speaking ran into a number of difficulties. Local variations of the language were one problem: to take a fairly basic example, the word house (or 'hyse' as Prince Charles and his friends pronounce it) can be correctly translated as either *tig* or *teach*.

Spelling was another problem. In 1962, the *Litriu Nua*, or New Spelling was introduced. It was designed to simplify the spelling of Irish words and bring them closer to the spoken form. The county of Leix, for example, which had become Laoighis in the early days of the State, now became Laois and the name Rory which used to be spelt Ruadhaire in Romanised Irish became Ruari in the new spelling. But the *Litriu Nua* did not come into full use until the 1970s and it caused a great deal of confusion as well as some resentment among purists who felt, with some justification perhaps, that there was no point in keeping a language alive if it meant changing it to such an extent that future generations would not be able to follow any of the ancient literature.

Another problem was that in the early days it was impossible to find enough teachers sufficiently fluent to teach Irish as a subject in itself, never mind enough teachers capable of using it as a vehicle for instruction in other subjects. In the first flush of enthusiasm, thousands of Irish teachers swotted up on their Irish and spent their holidays in the few Irish-speaking districts left, but there was a desperate shortage of stimulating books, and many of the teachers were too old to assimilate a new language anyway. The fact that secondary teachers got an extra ten per cent added to their salaries if they taught other subjects through the medium of Irish may have tempted many of them to claim a far higher degree of proficiency than they actually possessed. And this led to a situation in which teachers far from comfortably fluent in Irish spent their days trying to impart the intricacies of algebra and geometry in Irish, to English-speaking classes with only a very hazy knowledge of Irish themselves.

The accusation, though, that this situation produced a generation of people illiterate in two language is patently untrue. The hundreds of thousands of young Irish men and women who emigrated to the United States, the United Kingdom, and to other places in the English-speaking world – the doctors, engineers and scientists, as well as the building labourers and the barmen – found themselves at no marked disadvantage when they came up against their counterparts educated entirely in English.

Finally, the people who sneer at the Irish language and say that it is unfitted for general, everyday use in this highly technological twentieth century because words for commonly-used modern objects, such as telephones, fax-machines and PCs, have to be invented, are talking nonsense. New words had to be found for telephones and motor cars in all languages. The word 'transistor' couldn't exist, even in highly streamlined, up-to-the-minute English, until transistors themselves appeared on the scene.

There was, admittedly, a big back-log in the case of Irish, because for well over a hundred years – years which saw immense changes in the social and economic structure of the civilised world – the Irish language was spoken only in the Gaeltacht areas, where life was lived very much as it had been lived two or three centuries earlier. But this simply meant that instead of inventing new Irish words for things as they came along, the scholars could go back over the past few centuries to overhaul the vocabulary thoroughly, and fill in the gaps.

And although some civil service associations complained that the language tests not only failed in their purpose, but had even antagonised many people who would otherwise have been quite prepared to work for the language, Irish continues to be used sporadically in the civil service, sometimes, I'm told, as a form of one-upmanship, sometimes from a genuine love of the language. It also has its *pas devant* uses too; Irish ambassadors abroad have been known to use Irish as a sort of unofficial code when phoning headquarters in Dublin. And, as John Ardagh discovered, it has again become smart to take a pride in the language and lapse into it occasionally, just as it was in the 1890s when Douglas Hyde and Eoin MacNeill founded the Gaelic League and even the trend-setting George Moore (absentee landlord, bestselling author and society fop) contemplated learning the language in order to write the first bestseller in Irish.

Commands in the Irish Army were originally all in Irish and in the 1960s and 1970s a vigorous drive was made to introduce Irish as the main language of communication in the armed forces, but instructors got into terrible difficulties trying to explain the intricacies of new Swedish weapons in Irish, working from manuals translated from Swedish into obscure and incomprehensible English. Now that units of the Irish Army have served abroad in Cyprus and the Lebanon and the Congo, the emphasis on the use of Irish has been relaxed and odd phrases of Greek and Swahili are creeping into barrack-room slang, though Irish was widely used in the Congo as a military intelligence code in the 1960s.

The attempt to revive Irish by force as the standard, everyday language of the country started to grind to a halt in the 1960s. The Irish-speaking colleges which prepared students for careers as National School teachers, teaching through the medium, were phased out in the late 1950s and as early as 1961, the main opposition party, Fine Gael, included in its election manifesto a proposal to drop compulsory Irish. When Fine Gael came to power in a coalition in 1973, one of its first decisions was to remove a pass in Irish as a pre-requisite to the Leaving Certificate; at the same time the necessity for a pass in Irish, at Leaving Certificate standard, before entry into the civil service, was also abandoned.

These days the Government seems to have washed its hands of the whole idea of using any form of compulsion, or indeed any very strong initiative in restoring the Irish language as the first language of the State, and has left efforts to preserve what is left of it more and more to the language societies. There are about fifteen of these, including Douglas Hyde's Gaelic League and Gael Linn, a brash and bustling organisation which, since the 1960s, has been trying to spread Irish through the medium of Bingo, pop music, football pools and films. The various efforts of all the societies are co-ordinated by a government-sponsored body known as *Comhdail Naisiunta na Gaelige* (the National Council of the Irish Language), set up as a result of an early report by a Commission appointed to inquire into the best means of reviving the language.

In 1965, while I was in the council's offices in Dublin researching *The Irish Answer*, I came across two dictionaries which indicated the prodigious efforts that were then being made to boot the Irish language into the twentieth century. One was a dictionary of technical terms used in business, issued by the Irish Society of Certified Public Accountants. From it I learned that the Irish for final dividend is *dibhinn criochnaiheach* and that an undischarged bankrupt is a *feimbheach neamhdheimhnithe*. I remarked then, and I see no need to alter my opinion now, that it was a safe bet that English would remain the principal language of business in Ireland.

The other book on the desk in the room in which I was waiting was a then new official English-Irish dictionary compiled by Tomas de Bhaldraithe. Having found jet aircraft listed as *scaird-eitelean* and nuclear as *eithneach*, I grew bolder and more adventurous and went on to discover that birth control was translated as *cosc beireatais* and, even more surprisingly in view of the temper of the times, that contraceptive appeared as *frithghiniunt*. At this point the owner of the desk came back and I confessed to him what I had been up to and expressed surprise that anybody would go to the bother and trouble of inventing a word in Irish for a thing that was, and probably would always remain, unobtainable in Ireland, whatever language was used in any attempt to purchase it.

'Oh, I don't know so much about that,' he said, very prophetically as it has turned out. 'We're changing a lot in Ireland these days. And as soon as the Irish take a new idea on board, it doesn't take all that long for them to go overboard, along with it.'

Only about ten per cent of RTE (Radio Telefis Eireann) transmissions are in Irish, and although the company offers a twenty per cent discount to advertisers who elect to make commercials in Irish, there are not many takers. One advertising agent told *Irish Times* journalist Michael Viney: 'If a client suggested advertising in Irish, I'd try to talk him out of it. It's hard enough trying to sell Irish-made goods without using a language that most people don't understand.'

On the other hand, in one recent issue of the *Irish Times* (Saturday, 8 October 1994) I found three separate stories which would seem to indicate that interest in the Irish language is far from dead.

First there was a report that RTE has been authorised by the Minister for Arts, Culture and the Gaeltacht to start spending part of £3 million set aside for setting up an all-Irish television station, *Teilifis na Gaelige*, by appointing a director, news editors and other staff for the station. This announcement was greeted by Kevin Myers who writes the *Irishman's Diary* column in the same newspaper with a remark that *Teilifis na Gaelige*, which he rechristened Teilifis De Lorean, had about the same market potential as that ill-fated sports car, adding that it would cost £27 million to start up, and £20 million a year to run and noting that S4C, the Welsh language alternative to the ITV Channel 4, costs £40 million a year to run which works out at approximately £1,000 per viewer.

Then there was another story, by Uinsionn Mac Dubhghaill, Irish Language Editor of the newspaper – and the existence of such a post is yet another sign that the language, so far from being in its death throws, is alive and kicking – to the effect that the honorary secretary of the Unionist Party in Northern Ireland, Chris McGimpsey, had indicated that any future political settlement in Northern Ireland should include a firm recognition of the cultural and historical value of the Irish language. He said that a growing number of Unionists see the Irish language as 'part of a common heritage shared by both traditions' in Northern Ireland. The article reminded me of something I had perhaps forgotten – that until now Irish street names have been forbidden by law in Northern Ireland, and that the three all-Irish primary schools in the Six Counties, in Newry, County Down, Maghera, County Armagh and in Belfast, and the two all-Irish secondary schools in Belfast and Derry are not officially recognised as schools, and do not receive any government funding.

This story was followed a couple of weeks later by an announcement in the Church of Ireland Notes in the same newspaper that the Protestant Archbishop of Dublin was about to launch two liturgical books in Irish, one a volume of sacred music for choirs and the other a volume of collects for Sundays, principal holy days and seasons. The Church of Ireland and indeed all the other

Protestant churches in Ireland have always strongly supported the Irish language and, in general, the language has always been extremely well-taught in Protestant schools. At St Andrew's College, a Protestant secondary school run by a Presbyterian trust, my Irish master was Sean Kavanagh, known as Sean an Chota (John of the Coat), from Dunquin, County Kerry, a well-known authority on the Irish language, who was compiling a dictionary which, he once assured me, would supersede that of the Reverend Father Dineen. He never finished it for the very good reason that since he was being paid at what amounted to a piece rate, there was no pressing need for him ever to finish it. I lost touch with him, but I understand he had not got much beyond the letter 'G' when he died. I have been unable to check whether anybody else finished it, because nobody in Ireland seems to have heard of him.

The third story in that issue of the *Irish Times* was a paragraph in Renagh Holohan's Saturday *Quidnunc* column. She referred to a press hand-out from the Minister for Education, Niamh Bhreathnach, pointing out that the initial 'h' in her surname (used to indicate an accent which would be difficult to reproduce in type; the aspirate itself is used to indicate the genitive) is correctly there only when her surname is preceded by her first name. Headlines such as 'Bhreathnach says . . .' and the like are therefore incorrect, and should read 'Breathnach says . . .' Similarly, 'Ms Bhreatnach' is incorrect.

Renagh Holohan goes on: 'This begs the question: what is the best way to translate Ms into Irish? The traditional forms, *bean* [wife of] for a married woman or *inion* [daughter of] for an unmarried woman are sexist as they refer to the appellant's relationship to a man, her husband, or father. *Ceist duitse, a Aire.*' (Over to you, Minister, or more literally, a question for you, Minister.)

The very fact that a popular, liberated feminist and with-it weekend columnist thinks it worth her while to devote an entire paragraph to speculating about the politically correct form of Irish for 'Ms' is yet another indication that Irish once again is becoming fashionable among the smart set. And that, in the end, may be its very best hope of survival.

So while it seems that the results of over seventy years' efforts to revive Irish have succeeded in keeping the language alive and in fair health, it is now widely accepted that it will not and cannot ever replace or even supplement English on any serious scale as the main language of trade and commerce in Ireland. Whether the less fanatical, low-pressure approach of more recent governments, coupled with the efforts of organisations like Gael Linn, along with its recent re-adoption by the intellectuals as a slightly esoteric badge of distinction, will be any more successful in regaining all the ground lost by the doctrinaire dogmatists of the Gaelic League remains to be seen.

If they are not, a suggestion made in the 1960s might be worth considering as a last resort. A dentist from County Tipperary once confided to me confidently that 'in view of the general perversity of the Irish nation, myself included, there's only one way guaranteed to work. If they really want to revive the Irish language, all they have to do is ban it.'

9

A Torrent of Words

Irish and Anglo-Irish Literature

The Irish have rediscovered and revitalised their traditional music to such an extent that Irish groups like U2 now regularly head the charts, and pixilated back-packing teenagers from all over the world now go on pilgrimages to Ireland as the prime source and inspiration of a new and universal ethnic folk music. From time immemorial until a few years back, the Irishman, ancient or modern, has always been at his very best when handling words, written or spoken or sung or acted on the stage, or preached from a pulpit, or debated in a university; and the Irishman in this context includes the Anglo-Norman and the Gael, the layman and the cleric, the actor and the poet, the ballad singer and the television pundit, the politician and the man on the top of the Dalkey bus.

The earliest existing Irish literature dates from the sixth century AD. Written down by the early Christian monks, it includes versions of those heroic and semi-mythological sagas passed on in an oral tradition by the people who invaded Ireland in successive waves in the 50,000-odd years before the arrival of Saint Patrick, and prefaced by and in some cases interspersed with Christian accounts of the creation and other myths.

I have already referred to the *Tain Bo Cuailgne* (The Cattle Raid of Cooley) and the saga *Cath Maige Tured* (The Battle of Moytura). Other works of this period include the love stories of Diarmuid and Grainne, and of Deirdre and Naoise, believed by many authorities to be the principal source of the various versions of the saga of Tristan and Isolde, though I cannot for the life of me see why anything as basic as a straightforward heterosexual affair between a man and a woman requires any specific, artificial source other than common human experience.

Then there were narratives of voyages, like *Immram Curaig Maile Duin* (The Voyage of Mael Duin's boat) and the account (in Latin, unlike all the others) of St Brendan's trans-Atlantic adventures, *Navigatio Brendani*, as well as an account of Saint Patrick's journey throughout Ireland, written by Tirechan in the seventh century.

These books were written in what is known as Old Irish. Irish is divided into four linguistic periods: Old Irish, AD 700–950; Middle Irish, 950–1200; Early Modern, 1200–1650 and Late Modern, 1650 to the present time. I have taken these figures from *Ireland Since the Rising* (London, Pall Mall Press, 1966) by Tim Pat Coogan, who comments: 'Only fragments of old Irish exist in manuscript but, because of the unbalanced, over-romantic nature of the language revival in the nineteenth century, the usages of the other three periods were entwined in the vocabularies and dialects of the first Gaelic League teachers to spread the language. The results achieved often were akin to a blend of Chaucerian with contemporary English, with a whiff of the Anglo-Saxon Chronicle to add period flavour.'

Old Irish coincides with the troubled times when the Danes were constantly making raids on the country and looting the monasteries of their illuminated manuscripts and golden chalices and is generally regarded as a period of literary stagnation. Works produced during the Middle Irish Period include 150 cantos on biblical themes, such as *Saltair na Rann* (The Psalter of Verses) of 988 AD and the historical poems of Flann Mainistrech (*c.* 1000–56). There is also the *Dinnsenchas* (Placelore), a collection of verse and compilations of legends and speculations about famous places, and a satire on monks and literary men, *Aislinge Meic Conglinne* (The Dream of Mac Conglinne).

Following the social and political changes which resulted from the arrival of the Anglo-Normans in 1169, there begins what is known as Early Modern Irish language and literature. It is characterised by a more or less standard literary language, associated principally with the secular schools of language and literature which were maintained right up to the end of the seventeenth century by the professional – and often hereditary – poet-scholars. Known as *filidh* in Irish and bards in English, they were sponsored by those who survived of the ancient Celtic Irish chieftains and their successors, who sometimes pretended to have 'taken the porridge' (i.e., accepted the British bribes to turn Protestant after the Reformation) but who secretly had remained Catholic.

It was during the Early Modern period that the great oral cycle of the Fionn or Ossianic legends were first written down in full. As mentioned in chapter two on mythology, Fionn was the legendary leader of an ancient Irish Celtic warrior band, the Fianna; his son was called

Oisin. And although the first references to Fionn appear in manuscripts in the eighth and ninth centuries, the first full treatment of the cycle didn't emerge until the twelfth century.

Agallamh na Seanorach (The Conversation of the Old Men) consists of a compilation of prose tales and lyrical verse. The stories are linked together by the device of supposing that Oisin, the son of Fionn, with one of his comrades in arms, Caoilte, survived well into Christian times, met Saint Patrick and travelled the country with him, telling him tales about Fionn and the Fianna connected with all the places they visited together.

In the seventh-century account of Saint Patrick's journeys in Ireland by Tirechan, there is an interesting example of the juxtaposition of ancient myth and legend with the sterner realities of the Christian legacy. In one example, some disciples of Saint Patrick encounter a giant's grave, still common enough all over Ireland; this one was 125 feet long. The disciples went to the saint and told him that they were having great difficulties in accepting that a man of such an enormous size could possibly ever have lived; probably on the basis that if humans were made in the image of God, as the Good Book assures us all that we are, no single member of the human race could differ so profoundly in overall general dimensions from God's only human incarnation in the form of Jesus of Nazareth as this giant so obviously did. Patrick assured his disciples – who appear to have been every bit as gullible as other early Christian disciples – that a giant of such a size had indeed lived, once upon a time. He then silenced them further with the performance of a minor miracle in the course of which he opened up the giant's grave and resurrected him briefly, before baptising him and sending him back to his grave.

The Fenian cycle of legends has continued to inspire writers and poets right up to the present day: in 1750, Michael Coimin composed his *Laoi Oisin ar Thir na nOg* (Oisin's song about the Land of Youth) which was probably the last literary composition based on the cycle in Early Modern Irish, though W.B. Yeats, George Moore, AE (George Russell), Lady Gregory, J.M. Synge and other writers associated with the Irish Literary Revival at the beginning of the twentieth century were to carry excursions into this area of Irish mythology right into our own times, using a form of English which attempted to imitate the cadences of Irish. It was invented by Lady Gregory, and was known as Kiltartan, after a village near her home at Coole Park in County Sligo.

The Early Modern period came rapidly to an end after the Flight of the Earls and the overthrow of the old Ulster Catholic Celtic aristocracy in Elizabethan times, and the transition is marked by prose collections designed to preserve some records of the old Celtic civilisation. These include *Annala Ruighachta Eireann* (Annals of the Kingdom of Ireland), and Seathrun Ceitinn's narrative history, *Foras Feasa ar Eirinn* (Basic Knowledge about Ireland). Seathrun Ceitinn also wrote poetry, though during this period the patronage of poets and bards declined rapidly.

By the end of the eighteenth century literary patronage had disappeared altogether, a fact noted by one of the best-known poets of the period, Antoine O Reabhtabhra or, in the new spelling, Reachtaire (1784–1835), more widely known as Raftery:

I am Raftery the poet,
Look at me now,
My face to the wall,
Playing music
To empty pockets.

Probably the most successful of the poets of this period was a mathematics master, Brian Merriman (1747–1805), who wrote a lengthy poem *Cuirt an Mhean Oidche* ('The Midnight Court') which has attracted more translators than most other Irish poems, among them Frank O'Connor, whose version was banned for many years. The poem is a bitter satire in which the lusty women of Ireland castigate the men for their impotence and general lack of interest in sex, and openly rejoice in the fact that at least the priests are prepared to take advantage of the situation. It takes the form of a court case, in which first the women, and then the men, state their case. Here is a brief quotation from O'Connor's defence on behalf of the men of Ireland, which takes the form of a sad tale of deceit:

But I took it for talk and hardly minded
Sure a man like me could never be blinded –
And I smiled and nodded and off I tripped
Till my wedding night when I saw her stripped
And knew too late that this was no libel
Spread in the pub by some jealous rival –
By God, 'twas a fact, and well-supported
I was a father before I started!
So there it was in the cold daylight,
A family man, after one short night!

If Merriman is largely remembered because of Frank O'Connor's spicy rendition of his verse – and it is interesting that no Irish poet writing principally in Irish has ever been banned – Antoine o Reachtabhra, known as Raftery the poet, belonged to the strand of oral folk-poetry and owes his renown very largely to the rather sentimental *Songs Ascribed to Raftery*, published in 1903 by Douglas Hyde, who had gathered the material from oral sources. Douglas Hyde was also involved in the Irish Literary Revival around the turn of the century, which marked the point where two literary traditions – the ancient Celtic Irish and the Anglo-Irish – converged.

Since the Literary Revival, Irish writers have continued to write in Irish, and what is more, to find publishers prepared to print their work, another sign that Irish is far from being a dead language. Mairtin O Cadhain (1907–70) was probably the most productive and persistent champion of the Irish language in recent times. To quote Tim Pat Coogan: 'Some of O Cadhain's work, particularly *Cre na Cille* (The Dust of the Graveyard), a story in which the dead talk about their native village, would rank with either of these highly esteemed writers [Frank O'Connor and Sean O Faolain] in English. Before writers such as these came on the Irish literary scene, the major works in the language were written about what was practically a neolithic way of life. Three of such works reached international stature: *An t-Iolanach* (The Islander) by Tomas O Criomthain, *Fiche Bliain Ag Fas* (Twenty Years Agrowing) by Muiris O Suilleabhain and *Peig* by Peig Sayers.' All these books were based on life on the Blaskets (now uninhabited apart from Inishvicklane, the personal property of former Taoiseach Haughey) and the Aran Islands in Galway Bay.

Anglo-Irish Literature is probably a valid term to use to draw a distinction between English literature written by Englishmen and that written in English by Irish or Anglo-Irish authors. From William Molineaux's *The Case of Ireland Stated* (1698) to Conor Cruise O'Brien's *Ancestral Voices* (1994); from Jonathan Swift's *Gulliver's Travels* (1726) to Flann O'Brien's *At Swim-Two-Birds* (1939), or indeed, even to Roddy Doyle's *Paddy Clarke Ha ha ha* (1992), Anglo-Irish writing has always had a very distinctive character which could perhaps be partly explained by the fact that even if the writers did not speak Irish themselves, they were well aware of its existence as a separate and different language, and they were also very fully aware of the extravagant and picturesque use to which the English language was put by their Irish friends and neighbours.

And although Aogan O Rathaille and Jonathan Swift were contemporaries, their worlds hardly touched, as the 1989 edition of the excellent government publication, *Facts About Ireland*, puts it: 'And there is a plangent irony in the fact that one tradition was born while the other decayed. O Rathaille's theme was the decay of the old Gaelic Catholic order; Swift's was the humiliation of the Irish Protestant nation at the hands of the London Parliament. Neither writer ever heard the other's voice. Yet the development of an Irish literary tradition was to involve the mutual discovery and interpenetration of these two nations, their languages, aspirations and culture.'

The great eighteenth-century flowering of Anglo-Irish colonial literature was almost totally Protestant, and focused upon London and its clubs, theatres and town houses. This took place during the period when the

English comedy of manners, as it has been called, was dominated by Anglo-Irish playwrights like George Farquhar, William Congreve, Oliver Goldsmith and Richard Brinsley Sheridan. Their plays nearly always featured a bibulous, irascible, eloquent stage Irishman and they themselves had almost invariably been educated at Irish Protestant grammar schools and at Trinity College, Dublin.

Swift was different. As Dean of Saint Patrick's Cathedral in Dublin, he became passionately involved in Anglo-Irish politics. In his *Drapier's Letters* (1724), he put the Anglo-Irish case as forcibly as it has ever been put and attacked Westminster for imposing its will upon the Dublin Parliament.: 'Am I a free-man in England, and do I become a slave in six hours by crossing the channel?' he asked. And at a time when any suggestion of cannibalism raised very different feelings from the sort of reaction it arouses today, in the wake of various court cases and films like *The Silence of the Lambs*, he ironically suggested that more than at least two of the problems facing Ireland's native Irish population (too little money and too many children) might be solved if the native Irish were to sell their children for food. 'I have been assured', he wrote, in *A Modest Proposal for Preventing the Children of Ireland from Being a Burden to their Parents or Country*, 'by a very knowing American of my acquaintance in London, that a young, healthy child well nursed is at a year old a most delicious, nourishing and wholesome food, whether stewed, baked or boiled, and I make no doubt that it will equally serve as a fricassee, or a ragout.'

The new Protestant Patriot Parliament of the eighteenth century brought not only a new upsurge of political thought and oratory from people like Grattan, Flood and

John Philpot Curran, but also a revival of interest in the ancient Celtic literature. Charlotte Brooke's *Reliques of Irish Poetry* released glimpses of the old Ossianic poems, and Thomas Moore was at the same time setting new, romantic words to old Irish melodies. Some of the balladry of the Year of Liberty, the year of the 1798 rebellion, was fuelled by spin-offs from the French Revolution and the European Romantic movement in literature. However, in its aftermath, the new spirit of independence was very soon crushed by the Act of Union of 1800 which abolished the Irish Parliament (an aim that was very largely achieved by bribery on a massive scale, the cost of which was gratuitously added to the Irish National Debt) and, in the process, reduced Dublin's status from that of an independent capital city to that of a provincial town in a far from united kingdom of which London was the capital.

The literature of the period that followed the Union was dominated by Maria Edgworth, daughter of an Irish Protestant landlord, whose books *Castle Rackrent* (1800) and *The Absentee* (1812) addressed both the problem of Anglo-Irish identity and that of landlords torn between the lure of London and their responsibilities towards their tenants – a situation later re-examined by George Moore in such novels as *A Drama in Muslin*. Other Irish writers in this *genre* included Charles Lever and Samuel Lover, Elizabeth Bowen and that extremely witty double act, Somerville and Ross, who wrote *Some Experiences of an Irish RM* (Resident Magistrate). They were two Anglo-Irish gentlewomen, Edith Oenone Somerville and Violet Martin and, like Molly Keane more recently who initially wrote under the pseudonym of M.J. Farrell, they were obliged to pretend that they were men in order to get their work published.

The Irish Literary Revival is generally accepted as having sprung from a performance in Dublin of W.B. Yeats's *Countess Cathleen* and Edward Martyn's *The Heather Field* on a double bill in 1889. George Moore was involved to the extent that, as a friend of Martyn's with some experience of having had plays of his produced in London theatres, he had helped to cast and produce both plays.

Yeats's play, performed by English actors and actresses, explored an Irish theme – the mixed reactions of an Anglo-Irish countess to the disastrous Irish Famine – and for the first time, attempted to put in modern dramatic form some of the ancient Celtic attitudes to gods and devils, an endeavour which inevitably led to protests from the Catholic hierarchy and to riots in the theatre. Martyn's *The Heather Field* attempted to apply Ibsen's social realism to Irish rural life.

George Moore, already an established bestselling novelist in Britain, had initially intended to go to Ireland and learn Irish and write the first great novel himself in that language. But finding it a bit more difficult than he had expected, he had instead written a series of short stories for the Gaelic League to translate into Irish. These stories, re-translated back into English by the Gaelic League, and yet again refurbished by Moore, and then republished in England under the title of *The Untilled Field*, were extremely successful, as indeed dramatisations of some of them have recently proved to be on RTE (Radio Telefis Eireann).

George Moore also profited from his *séjour* in Ireland by writing his own, highly-personalised account of the Irish Literary Revival in the form of three semi-autobiographical volumes collectively entitled *Hail and Farewell*;

the individual volumes, which came out separately – though none until after 1910, when Moore had left Ireland for the safety of Ebury Street in London – were entitled *Ave*, *Salve* and *Vale*.

However, despite the fact that Moore soon lost all interest in it as soon as the final volume of his trilogy had been published, the Irish Literary Revival prospered and settled down in the form of the Abbey Theatre, founded in 1903 by a wealthy Manchester heiress, Mrs Annie Frederika Horniman, and the Fay brothers, the actor-managers of the Irish Literary Theatre Society. The Abbey was soon fostering a new generation of Irish playwrights, notably Yeats himself, Lady Gregory, J.M. Synge, whose *Playboy of the Western World* took an uncomfortably candid look at Irish peasant girlhood in Connemara and caused a celebrated riot in 1907, and Sean O'Casey, whose cynicism about the Irish fight for freedom led to another notable riot in the 1920s.

In the meantime, Irish playwrights had continued, if not to dominate, at any rate to make a very considerable mark upon the English theatre. After Congreve and Sheridan and the first wave of Irish playwrights came Dion Boucicault with his, for the period, extremely trendy Irish melodramas like *The Colleen Bawn* and *The Shaugraun*; Oscar Wilde with his dazzling displays of verbal athletics; and George Bernard Shaw with his shatteringly sensible and surprisingly entertaining sermons on various aspects of Socialism. Between them all, they delighted several generations of London theatre-goers.

And although the Abbey Theatre has not produced much in the way of theatrical genius in recent years, Irish playwrights have continued to capture the headlines in the West End of London and on and off Broadway. The big hits have included Samuel Beckett's *Waiting for Godot*; Brendan Behan's *The Hostage* and *The Quare Fella*; as well as plays like Thomas Murphy's *Whistle in the Dark*, Brian Friel's *Philadelphia, Here I Come!* and *Dancing at Lughnasa*, and Hugh Leonard's *Da*. Leonard also had a success in London's West End with an adaptation of James Joyce's *A Portrait of the Artist as a Young Man*, which was transferred to the stage as *Stephen D*. It is perhaps worth noting here that some of Behan's first plays, notably *The Hostage*, were originally written in Irish. And although Yeats's plays are rarely performed these days, he emerged from the so-called 'Celtic Twilight' as one of the greatest lyric poets of his time, if not of all time.

With his fantasy *The Crock of Gold*, James Stephens opened up a new and curiously distinctive Irish vein of humour, later more fully exploited by an Irish civil servant, Briain O Nuallain, writing in Irish and English as Myles ne gCopaleen, subsequently, out of deference to his mainly English-speaking readers, simplified into Myles na Gopaleen (it means Myles of the Little Horse), in his column *Cruiskeen Lawn* (it means full jug) in the *Irish Times*, and in English as Flann O'Brien, the novelist and author of *At Swim-Two-Birds*, *The Dalkey Archive* and *The Third Policeman*.

Myles freely acknowledged the debt he owed to the ancient Celtic tradition. When the *Irish Times* published the first paperback collection of extracts from his column and asked him for some suggestions for the cover, he came up with the idea of a spoof *Irish Times* front page, with an eight-column banner headline announcing: MYLES NA GOPALEEN CROWNED KING OF IRELAND. Other headlines in that splendid front page read: HISTORIC

SCENE AT TARA; STIRRING MESSAGE TO NATION; DAIL DISSOLVED BY ROYAL DECREE: and NEW MONARCH'S SWIFT STROKE – SPEAKING OF ENGLISH PROHIBITED.

He had even gone to the trouble of writing the introductions to some of the stories in what was a brilliant parody of Irish journalese of that period. One began:

> The ancient glories of Erin were revived yesterday, when Mr Myles na Gopaleen, the famous scholar, wit and authority on patent cattle drench, was crowned King of All Ireland on historic Tara Hill. A day of brilliant pageantry culminated in the solemn coronation ceremonies, which were conducted throughout in Middle Irish. The sea-divided Gael was in evidence on all sides, eighteen special trains being run from Liverpool.

Myles's subtitle for that collection of extracts was written in Irish, with each Irish word followed, in brackets, by a translation into English. The English version read as follows:

> Extracts from the daily labours of the wise man, Myles na Gopaleen, presented here, safe from extinction and eternal loss through the kindly leave of the persons conducting the *Irish Times*.

James Joyce, who published his first work, a book of poems called *Chamber Music* in 1907, left Ireland as a very young man and spent the rest of his life abroad, mainly in Paris, Zurich and Trieste. Initially supporting himself by teaching English, he went on to create a body of prose that was to revolutionise the English language novel form, notably in *Ulysses* (1922), a stupefyingly intense account of one day in Dublin shortly after the turn of the century (16 June 1904) and *Finnegan's Wake* (1939). Of the latter, the *Irish Times* commented that having said all that could possibly be said in *Ulysses*, James Joyce continued saying it in *Finnegan's Wake*. His one-time secretary, Samuel Beckett, went on to explore various bleak aspects of the cul-de-sac of human bafflement and utter despair in his plays like *Waiting for Godot* and novels like *Murphy*, *Malloy*, *Malone Dies* and *Unnameable*.

And any list of leading contemporary novelists and short-story writers, judged on any basis whatsoever, would have to include a disproportionate number of Irish names, among them Edna O'Brien and Maeve Binchy, William Trevor and Brian Moore, Jennifer Johnston and James Plunkett, John Banville and John McGahern, Thomas Murphy and Roddy Doyle. I could go on and on indefinitely, but what's the point in printing lists of anything?

The point that makes itself is that in the business of communication, Saint Patrick's people have, over the centuries, proved themselves second to none.

10

Magic of a Very High Order

Art and Architecture

The earliest inhabitants of Ireland were shore-dwelling fisherfolk and hunters and gatherers who left no structures or artefacts behind them, and no evidence of their presence other than small scraps and shards unearthed by the spades of the archaeologists during the last century.

But the Bronze Age farmers who followed them about 3,000 BC had brought with them from the shores of the Mediterranean various rites and customs which demanded the construction of huge, elaborate structures for disposing of and, in the process, honouring their dead. I touched on the subject of Ireland's megalithic tombs in the first chapter of this book. The most remarkable of them all, the cluster of passage-graves at Newgrange in the Boyne Valley in County Meath, is probably the most sophisticated monument of its kind in Northern Europe, if not in the world, and it merits a closer look.

If you can bring yourself to ignore the Disneyland flavour of the entrance, recently rebuilt after extensive excavations in the 1960s and 1970s and jazzily clad in a façade of dazzling white quartz which may or may not have been used on the façade of the original megalithic tumulus, you will find yourself confronted with, as Michael Jenner puts it in *Ireland Through the Ages* (London: Michael Joseph, 1992), 'a wild but confident array of spirals . . . this is no haphazard doodling, but one of the great works of European prehistoric art. We may understand the swirling designs how we will.' They have been interpreted as everything from a local map of the Boyne Valley's main tombs to an image of the universe, as symbols of the supplies of underground water available in that area to a diagrammatic abstraction of the afterlife. 'The power of the composition is overwhelming,' he goes on, 'with its mystifying triple spiral which suggests a seamless vortex of life force, without beginning or end, which is far beyond anything that our present binary perception of reality can properly comprehend.'

But even if you do not feel inclined to go along with all that extremely high-falutin' stuff, you can hardly fail to be impressed by the knowledge that when you penetrate sixty feet into the mound and reach the central, cruciform chamber, you are in a scientifically-designed location, naturally illuminated only once a year and for approximately seventeen minutes on a few days in the middle of December as a fanlight over the entrance, known as the roofbox, catches the first rays of the rising sun of the winter solstice.

This is generally believed to have been used as a magical sign by the Druids, or their Bronze Age predecessors, some time around 2000 BC, who might have interpreted it as an indication from the gods that the turning-point in the long, dark winter had finally been reached, possibly by employing the symbolism of the penetration by a solar shaft of this megalithic womb, which they could have presented as the fertilisation of mother earth by the sun god himself, though how they managed to demonstrate this aspect of their magic to more than a tiny sample of their clients, in view of all the problems associated with getting more than about a dozen people into the central chamber without any major disasters, even now remains one of the many unsolved mysteries associated with Newgrange. The biggest mystery of all is, of course, how they managed to build such a scientifically precise and accurate instrument of measurement using only lumps of rock.

In the earliest Celtic myths, Newgrange features as the abode of many of the gods, and was referred to in Irish as *Uaimh na Greine*, the cave of the sun. Later it was claimed to be the ancestral burial place – in the sense of a repository for the ashes, since cremation was customary at this period – of the High Kings of Tara; it is only about ten miles from the former seat of the kings. Nearby, there are two other similar cairns – artificial hills built over the tombs – at Dowth and Knowth. They each cover more than an acre of ground, and are all sited within the same bend of the Boyne river, near Navan.

Tombs are not the only prehistoric megalithic structures in Ireland. Isolated standing stones and rings of standing stones, like Stonehenge, though not on the same scale, are quite numerous. According to archaeologist Liam de Paor writing in *Ireland* (edited by Owen Dudley Edwards, London: André Deutsch, 1969) they were probably open-air temples. Some of these stone circles were still being erected in Christian times, De Paor claims, as indicated by what he calls the 'conversion' of some of them by means of the addition of an engraved Christian-type cross.

The final wave of Celts who arrived in Ireland around 300 BC came from the La Tene cultural period, so called after La Tene in today's Switzerland, where it originated, and although some specimens of Celtic metalwork of high quality have been found in limited areas of the country, in Ulster and around the Shannon river, the hill-forts which constituted the great tribal centres of the Celtic tribes in Britain and in Gaul are relatively few in number in Ireland and appear to have had a ritual rather than a defensive role.

Saint Patrick brought to Ireland with him not only a team of missionaries, scribes and teachers but also a company of artists and craftsmen which included Bishop Assicus, a brass-worker, according to the Book of Armagh. It informs us that Saint Patrick took with him to the far side of the Shannon a collection of bells, patens, chalices, altars, law-books and gospels for use in the churches he founded there.

The principal product of Saint Patrick and his scribes was the series of manuscripts through which all our knowledge of manners and customs and events in pre-Christian Ireland has been conveyed to us. These were written in a graceful script based on a form of Roman lettering very widely used at that time to write down the Franco-Lombardic oral sagas. This script was also used to teach the Irish how to read and write in their own language, and was exported with the Irish Saints and Scholars to Lindisfarne and other English monastic settlements and then further afield to the European mainland.

The Book of Kells is the best known of all the old Celtic manuscripts. It gets its name from the monastery of Kells, in County Meath, about forty miles (seventy kilometres) from Dublin, which became a refuge for followers of Saint Colum Cille (or Columba, in Latin) in flight from the Viking attacks on the island of Iona and where, it is generally assumed, it was completed. It dates from the sixth century AD and consists principally of the Latin text of the four gospels, featuring, among other things, a genealogy of Christ, portraits of Saint Matthew, Mark, Luke and John, both in their own right, so to speak, as apostles, and in the symbolic forms they took in the early church, with Matthew depicted as a man, emphasising the human side of Christ; Saint Mark portrayed as a lion, to stress Christ's power and royal dignity; Saint Luke represented as the sacrificial calf, to underline the priestly aspect of the incarnation; and St John in his role as the Eagle Evangelist, soaring to Heaven to peer into the blinding light of the Revelations. It also includes several very mundane documents in Irish, referring to grants of land from King Melaghin of Meath to the Abbey of Kells, the Bishop of Meath and the Church of Kells, dated between 1024 AD and the twelfth century. These were probably inserted between the pages of the Book of Kells by the monks for safe keeping. They are believed to be the only extant specimens of legal deeds in the Irish language dating back to before the Norman invasion.

Legend has it that this highly decorated – 'illuminated' is the word normally used – version of the Four Gospels was started by Saint Columba and the monks of the monastery at Iona, and was completed at Kells after the

Viking attacks on Iona in 806 AD. It was stolen, apparently for the sake of its gold-studded cover, when the monastery at Kells was in turn sacked by the Vikings during the tenth century, and the fact that some of the decorations were unfinished at the time it was stolen is used by many scholars to argue that this was because the monks were interrupted while still at work on the book.

It was eventually restored to the monastery, minus its gold cover, and when, during King Henry VIII's dissolution of the monasteries, the Abbey at Kells was surrendered to the Crown by its last Abbot, Richard Plunkett, the manuscript found its way into the hands of a Gerald Plunkett of Dublin, probably a relation of the Abbot's. While it was briefly in his possession, he annotated it – in exactly the same way as people today scribble remarks in the margins of library books – and many of his notes are still legible on the edges of the manuscript.

When James I ordered the collection of all antiquities connected with the Church, the Book of Kells was handed in to the appropriate authorities and eventually wound up in the library of Trinity College, Dublin. Today it is still on view, one page turned over every day, so that it would take you about a year to see the entire book, which consists of 340 folios (680 pages) of calf-skin vellum and measures 330 by 250 millimetres. With the possible exception of the Book of Lindisfarne, also the work of Irish scribes, it is widely accepted as the most beautiful example of Celtic manuscript illumination and illustration in the world.

As well as the illuminated manuscripts, the Celtic legacy has left us a collection of marvellous metalwork, now mostly in Ireland's National Museum in Kildare Street, Dublin, which includes the eighth-century Tara brooch made of silver gilt with gold filigree, amber and glass ornamentation; the Ardagh Chalice; and the Cross of Cong, a shrine fashioned in the eleventh century, by order of the High King, to house a fragment of the true cross which had contrived, somehow or another, to find its way to Ireland. Part of the National Museum's collection is shortly to be moved to Collins Barracks on the River Liffey near Phoenix Park, where there is far more room to show many more exhibits, including items which have been in storage for years. Collins Barracks – an old British army barracks, named after Michael Collins and used during the Emergency as a special criminal court for the trial of offences against the state – is currently being refurbished for the purpose.

Other examples of art and architecture from this period include stone sculptures, such as the High Cross at Carndonagh, and many of the stone crosses all over the country depicting scenes from the New Testament. There is also what remains of the early Christian Celtic monastic settlements like Glendalough, County Wicklow, Clomacnoise, County Offaly and Kells in County Meath, as well as a scattering of carvings collectively known as *Sheila-na-gCioch* (normally pronounced Sheila Na Gig), which depict an earth-goddess, one presumes, exposing her most private parts in a profane, if not obscene, manner, probably as a symbol of fertility.

And after that, there is almost nothing. Following the Norman invasion, most of Saint Patrick's people were far too busy, over the centuries, trying to keep body and soul together, to think about putting chisel to stone, or brush to paper.

The Anglo-Norman invaders – or, more accurately, the Cambrian-Norman invaders, since the first wave of them came from Wales – set about consolidating their hold on the country by erecting a string of feudal forts such as Cahir Castle in County Tipperary, cathedrals like Jerpoint Abbey and St Canice's, in County Kilkenny, there because Kilkenny was where the first Irish Parliaments sat. They were all built to the standard Norman design, but featured details that were unmistakably Celtic, probably because most of the stonemasons, joiners, master carpenters and other craftsmen they employed on the building sites were Irish Celts.

Meanwhile, the peasant Irish themselves were developing their own distinctive brand of architecture, represented by the traditional thatched cottage: four stout walls to keep out the wind, lime-washed, for hygiene and simplicity, with a couple of small windows to let in a bit of daylight and a thatched roof of reeds or whatever was ready to hand. Not great architecture in any sense, but possessing something of the same empathy with the landscape, the same indigenous character which so distinguishes the farm houses of Tuscany and the perched, hilltop villages, mainly composed of tiny hovels, of the Alpes-Maritimes and Provence.

Tomas O Criomhthain (in modern spelling Tomas O Crohan) who was born in just such a cottage on the Great Blasket Island off the coast of County Kerry, on St Thomas's Day in the year 1856, has left us a good description of the interior (taken from *An t-Oi-leanach*, translated as *The Islandman* by Robin Flower and published by Penguin Books in 1943, when the Blaskets were still inhabited and life was not greatly different from what he describes). He says he can recall being at his mother's breast, for he was four years old when he was weaned, and he remembers the surroundings in which he spent his childhood thus: 'We lived in a cramped little house, roofed with rushes from the hill. Often the hens would nest in the thatch and lay a dozen eggs there. We had a post-bed in the corner, and two beds at the bottom of the house. There used to be two cows in the house, the hens and their eggs, the ass and the rest of us.'

Later in the same book, he goes into more detail about the sort of houses the islanders inhabited until the islands were evacuated in the 1950s: 'A number of them were only ten feet by eight. Others were larger – from that size to fifteen or twenty feet long. To divide the house into two, a dresser stood out from the wall in the middle of the floor, and a partition met it from the other side. There were two beds in one portion, where people slept. Potatoes would be stored under these beds. A great chest was kept between the two beds, up against the gable end. On the other side of the partition – the kitchen side – the family used to spend the whole day, or part of the day, ten of them perhaps. There was a coop against the partition with hens in it, and a broody hen just by it, in an old cooking pot. At night-time, there would be a cow or two, a calf or two, the ass, the dog on a chain by the wall or running about the house. In a house with a large family you would find a post-bed, or maybe a bed on the floor. The old people used to spend the night in that [bed] beside the fire, with an old stump of a clay pipe going, or two pipes if there were two of them living, and smoking away...'

The gradual eclipse of the old Celtic Irish aristocracy eventually wiped out the ancient system of patronage under which Irish poetry and art had flourished. Guilds of urban craftworkers began to emerge, under strong

English and continental influence; and the new ruling class started to commission portraits of itself from the painters and sculptors. By the seventeenth century, the decorative arts of the goldsmith, the master-plasterer and the silver, glass and furniture craftsmen were firmly established under the auspices of English-orientated guilds such as the Goldsmiths of Dublin.

Easel-painting, as it was then called, replaced the arts of wall painting and tapestry and a painters' guild was formed in Dublin in 1670, and such painters as eventually developed from this guild stemmed entirely from the British tradition.

The glories of Georgian Dublin can claim very few Irish connections apart from the happy accident of Dublin's situation, with the mountains behind its back, and the sea spread out at its feet, for which no section of the community can claim any credit; but such buildings as the Royal Hospital at Kilmainham, built by one of the viceroys, the Duke of Ormonde, to house veterans of the British wars of conquest, was inspired by Les Invalides in Paris. And Edward Lovett Pearce's Parliament House in Dublin – 'Tell us what that pile contains?' asked Dean Swift, answering himself: 'Many a head that holds no brains' – which is now the headquarters of the Bank of Ireland, was plainly based on an English model, as were James Gandon's Four Courts and Customs House buildings which show clear signs of the influence of Sir Christopher Wren. Lord Charlemont, head of the Protestant Irish Volunteers at the time of Grattan's Parliament, not only built the noble town house which now exhibits the Hugh Lane Collection of Impressionist paintings and many other examples of modern art, but also a miniature neo-classical 'doll's house' in Clontarf known as the Marino Casino. The Municipal Gallery, Charlemont House and the Casino are connected by a tunnel, over a mile long, which Lord Charlemont had constructed for his own convenience, so that he could get from his home to his villa in privacy and without getting his head (or his feet) wet. A large section of the tunnel remains intact but it is closed because the heavy city traffic passing over it today has made it dangerous.

The greatest triumph of Georgian architecture lay in the squares and streets of uniformly designed and built town-houses of bricks and mortar, which all had individual and very stylish fan-lights and porches. When they were built, all the doors in any one street or square were painted the same colour – the writer, George Moore, caused a terrible furore which only stopped short of physical violence when he insisted on painting his front door at No. 4 Ely Place green instead of the customary white – but nowadays one of the most attractive features of Dublin's Georgian doorways is the wide range of bright and imaginative colours in which they are painted.

These houses were initially built for the people who worked directly and indirectly for the Dublin Parliament, and after the Act of Union of 1800, when Britain decided that Ireland could be more conveniently managed from Westminster, and the Members of Parliament and their camp-followers started to rent houses in London, many of them degenerated into the slums made famous in O'Casey's plays; others became doctors' and dentists' consulting rooms, or were turned into offices. Some idea of what Dublin must have looked like before the Act of Union killed off the Irish Parliament can be gained from James Malton's *Views of Dublin*, drawn in the 1790s and published as a very popular series of engravings.

During the years of what is called easel-painting, Ireland produced a few very competent portrait painters, among them John B. Yeats, father of the poet, William Butler, as well as William Orpen and John Lavery; a couple of competent landscape and *genre* painters including Nathaniel Hone and Walter Osborne; one distinguished dabbler in an elegant but narrow vein of modernism, Louis Le Brocquy; and one great painter, Jack B. Yeats, son of the portrait painter, John B., and brother of the poet W.B.

Jack Yeats painted huge, turbulent, dazzling pictures, squeezing the pigment straight from the tubes and spreading it across his canvasses with a palette knife in what seemed at times to be a frenzy of imaginative excitement. The poet Patrick Kavanagh, briefly employed as art critic by one of the Dublin literary reviews, made a comment to the effect that if anybody was to be congratulated for the success of Jack Yeats's pictures, it should be the oil paint manufacturers, Windsor and Newton, since he applied their colours straight from the tube.

His pictures were very strange. He once remarked to me that he never painted strange paintings, though it sometimes happened that what was in his mind was strange. And in later years he painted entirely from memory, or from imagination. He never used a model, and never painted from nature, but always from the interior of his own mind, and he normally worked with a single rose pinned to his easel. He was never particularly well known outside Ireland because he never allowed any colour reproductions to be made of his paintings, though he did have a very big exhibition of his work during his lifetime, in Paris.

He was certainly one of Saint Patrick's people in the

sense that his pictures were full of folk images. He would paint the interior of a cottage in Connemara, with a fairly normal view out of the window on to the Atlantic Ocean and the distant Aran islands, with maybe a tree outside in the yard and a chair somewhere near the half-door of the cottage. You would glance away from the canvas for a second, and by the time you had looked back at it, the chair near the door had become a mocking, dancing clown, and the tree outside had turned into a menacing, laughing tinker on a prancing horse. Armies of ancient warriors clashed in the clouds above the horizon and the distant islands had become great fleets locked together in deadly combat on the high seas, or Saracen pirates, raking the oceans for booty.

You had only to shake your head again for an instant, and the vision would dissolve and settle down and resolve itself once more into the chair by the cottage door, with the tree just outside it and that glimpse of the Atlantic in the background, which is all that you imagined you saw when you looked at the painting in the first place.

It was magic of a very high order.

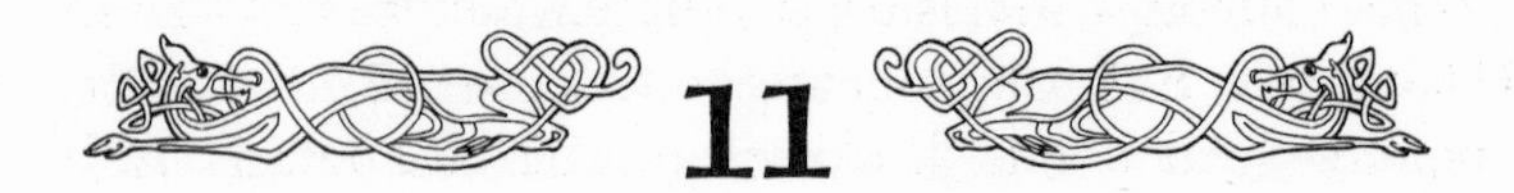

11

The Inner Irishman

Food and Drink

If the cultivation of grain can be regarded as a substantial step along the road to civilisation, then it is possible that the nature of the grain which was cultivated by the ancestors of the Irish Celts to some extent determined the nature of the ensuing civilisation.

In the case of the Irish Celts, it was oats, the only grain crop rugged enough to thrive in the relentless dampness of the Irish climate. And about the only thing you can do with oats is to make porridge, or a sort of rough, oatmeal bread with it. The rank and file of the Celtic ancestors of the Irish people appear to have existed almost entirely on porridge (enlivened occasionally by the addition of some honey) and from a kind of bread made from oatmeal, cheering up these dull but worthy repasts with draughts of mead, which was made from fermented honey, and beer which was brewed by the housewives; though the captains and the kings feasted on salmon, venison, wild boar, hare and beef, and drank Spanish wine.

In more recent times, the Anglo-Irish landlord classes

lived in more or less the same way as the landed gentry lived in England, and consumed roughly the same sort of food and drink. The plain people of Ireland, as the *Irish Times* columnist Myles na gCopaleen used to call them, kept body and soul together on the standard diet of potatoes and point, drinking only tea, buttermilk and water. It was not, in fact, a bad diet – low in cholesterol and sufficiently nourishing to produce a people capable of building railroads right across the North American continent – but not one out of which a rich, traditional, gourmet cuisine was likely to evolve.

And when, in the first quarter of this century, the Irish managed to achieve the freedom to run their own affairs in twenty-six of their thirty-two counties, there were far more pressing matters to concern them than the choice of food and drink. And although the Irish were always prepared to go to the furthest ends of the earth to look for work – or to preach the gospel or teach or minister to the sick in missionary hospitals or international relief agencies – most of them did not start going abroad for holidays until well after the Second World War, and few could afford to tour extensively until the boom-time of the middle 1960s.

In the circumstances, it is perhaps not surprising that the food they ate, to put it at its best, was on the unimaginative side. A passionate interest in food has never been a salient feature of the Irish character. There have, however, recently been signs of a slight awakening of interest in food: perhaps as part of the general pattern of increased affluence, and a direct result of package-tour holidays in France and Spain and Italy, plus the spread of expense-account entertainment, and as an incidental consequence of restaurants and hotels being forced to provide edible meals for the sake of the tourists. The latest spin-off from this tendency is Ballymaloe House, near Cork, a mansion with a 400-acre farm where Ivan and Myrtle Allen provide meals which have earned their restaurant all the Michelin stars and Euro-toques going. Their recipe for success is based on good old-fashioned farm cooking, without a hint of the *cuisine minceur*. And they have even found the native Irish perfectly willing to pay the £30 apiece that their fixed dinner costs, excluding wine.

But this new interest in food is something that has been tacked on to the Irish character; it is not an integral part of it. Even today, the average Irishman doesn't much care what he eats, so long as there is enough of it, and a farmer will make his dinner, happily, day after day, on boiled potatoes, smothered in butter, and washed down with milk or buttermilk. Pleasant enough, once in a while, but a little bit monotonous as a daily diet.

It is not in any way strange that a nation so undiscriminating about food has never developed anything outstanding in the way of a traditional cuisine. Nor is it very surprising that a people who for two or three centuries lived on the very edge of starvation should not be over-fussy about the kind of food they eat.

There used to be a firmly-rooted notion in America that the Irish traditionally eat corned beef and cabbage. Indeed, all the supermarkets in the States advertise corned beef and cabbage as a national speciality around Saint Patrick's Day. Traditionally, the Irish exported almost all of their beef, except what little was held back to grace the tables of the local gentry. When times were good, an occasional pig might be killed to vary the diet; so that boiled bacon (not corned beef) and cabbage could claim to be one of the very few traditional Irish dishes. It can be quite good, too, though it has unpleasant side-effects; the cabbage always makes a terrible smell during the cooking which clings to the house, and the clothes, for hours.

Drisheens – a sort of haggis, or white pudding, made from the innards of the pig – and crubeens, or pig's feet, are two obvious by-products of the beast that went into the bacon and cabbage, and are traditionally Irish to the extent that they were certainly eaten in Ireland, though they are also eaten elsewhere, as is black pudding, made largely from pig's blood. Stirrabout (porridge) is probably more Scottish than Irish, though it is one of the few Celtic staple foods specifically referred to in the old manuscripts. It is still eaten, probably increasingly reluctantly, at breakfast-time, by Irish children who on the whole now far prefer breakfast cereals like corn flakes or rice crispies.

Colcannon (mashed potatoes, flavoured with chopped greens, usually curly kale, and onions and served with a dollop of butter) represents an enterprising effort to do something different with potatoes; potato cakes and boxty, a sort of potato pie not unlike the English 'bubble and squeak', are other traditional variations on the potato theme, though again probably Scottish in origin; and barm brack, a brown, sweet currant bread not fundamentally different from some of the varieties of currant bread found in lots of places, may have originated in Ireland; the Gaelic word *breac* means speckled. Irish soda bread is good, but again no different from many other peasant breads of the same type. However, most Irish women know how to make brown (wholemeal) bread and white soda bread, made with buttermilk, and in general even factory bread in Ireland has far more flavour than the British all-plastic loaf.

Irish stew, which according to many authorities originated in Liverpool, was simply an effort to disguise an inferior cut of meat, or eke out an uncommonly small amount of it, or both, and hardly qualifies for consideration as a regional speciality, since similar stews are made in many other countries. And there is only one traditional Irish sweet: a sort of salty jelly made from a type of indigenous Irish seaweed known as Carrageen Moss. It is bland, tastes vaguely of the sea and is supposed to be good for a wide variety of human ailments, possibly on the principle that anything that has such an unpleasant taste must be good for you.

And that's about it. Enterprising chefs employed by Irish hotels and restaurants sometimes come up with fake regional specialities like 'Pancakes Colleen' or 'Volaille à l'Irlandaise', but seasoned travellers will immediately recognise them as permutations of familiar international dishes.

In the average middle-class home, meals used to follow the well-established English pattern: porridge or corn flakes followed by bacon and eggs for breakfast; a joint of roast beef with two veg. for Sunday lunch; rissoles or other made-up dishes from the left-overs for supper and for lunch on the following day; stews and fries for lunch for the rest of the week; and fish on Fridays. The evening meal almost always used to consist of tea, bread and butter, and sometimes included cold meat and salad or baked beans on toast, or a savoury dish of that sort.

Most Irishmen, even in the cities and towns, take time off to go home for their lunch (still normally called dinner, as it is in many parts of Britain); and travelling home during the lunch break didn't present any insurmountable problems, even in Dublin, until fairly recently. For nearly twenty years now, the traffic has made it impracticable for Dubliners even to consider going home for lunch. In any event, changes in life style, adopted as readily in Dublin as elsewhere, have made working and business lunches more popular.

The Irish make great tea and terrible coffee, but that probably has something to do with the water, because in recent years in Dublin City, where the water has to be heavily treated with chemicals, as it is in most cities, the coffee is steadily getting better and the quality of the tea is gradually deteriorating. But tastes are changing rapidly in Ireland, as they are everywhere else. Thirty years ago, there was only one genuine delicatessen in Dublin; now there are dozens, and every supermarket carries a wide range of exotic comestibles from the far corners of the earth. The same thing applies to drink. Thirty years ago the Irish mostly drank tea, milk, buttermilk or water with their meals; the bottle of Power's Gold Label whiskey on the sideboard was strictly for the parish priest, in case he happened to drop by. All the serious drinking was done in the pub.

Now you are quite likely to find a bottle of wine on the table, though wine remains prohibitively expensive as a result of government taxing policies. But most of the wine on sale in Ireland is very good, far better than the lower-priced plonks from the Roussillion or the Ardèche available in Britain; the Irish do not sell or drink what is known in France as château-tank, a mixture of the dregs of the wine lake and whatever chances to come up, by tanker, from Algeria. It could be that ancient ancestral associations with some of the noblest vintages (Lynch-

Bages, Kirwan etc.) have left the Irish with a better nose, as the wine-buffs say, than the British.

And the plain, red, cheddar-type cheese, which used to be the principal if not the only Irish variety, and which was usually referred to as 'rat trap' or 'mouse trap', has been ousted by a staggering variety of cheeses from all over the world, a lot of them now reproduced in Ireland. And these days, hardly a week goes by without some new and highly adventurous Irish cheese coming on the market; the better-known ones include Knockalara from County Waterford, Manch from Dunmanway in County Cork and Cashel Blue from County Tipperary. There is also an Irish feta cheese known as Drumiller from Dromore in Northern Ireland, and the several varieties of Irish-made versions of Brie and Camembert which are available compare very favourably with the French originals.

Wine consumption has more than doubled over the past ten years, and is now increasing at an average rate of ten per cent per year, with the supermarkets reporting annual increases of between twenty and thirty-five per cent for their wine departments. This indicates an entirely new level of demand for wine in Ireland and is almost entirely the result of holidays spent abroad and changing shopping habits of the Irish housewife. Everywhere in Ireland today, the supermarket has replaced the old-fashioned family shop, which was part-grocery, part-pub; you could order your groceries at one end of the shop and nip down the other end for a jar, while the order was being made up.

'In the old days, everything used to be kept under the counter or away at the back of the shop, and you had to order whatever you wanted by name,' a Wicklow woman remarked to me. 'And the result was that you only asked for things you were already familiar with. Now, with everything spread out on the shelves in front of your face, you can ferret around and find things for yourself. I'm always bringing home fresh foreign things to try out.'

But if Ireland has not produced any great gastronomical speciality to tickle the palates of the world's gourmets, it has certainly made the grade with a couple of drinks.

Guinness, that bitter, black stout with a creamy head of foam, is famous the world over; a pint of the stuff, showing the correct amount of white collar above the rich black of the vest, used to be known in the country as 'a parish priest'. Contrary to the widespread belief, it is not brewed from Liffey water, but with water from a spring in County Kildare, allegedly radio-active, which is why, Dubliners say, that the Guinness brewed anywhere else tastes quite different.

For over two centuries, stout has been made at St James's Gate Brewery in Dublin. It was on sale in London as early as 1794, the year Robespierre went to the guillotine in Paris. By Dickens's time, Guinness was sufficiently well known to be featured in an illustration for *The Pickwick Papers*. As early as 1815 it had reached Belgium; one of Wellington's cavalry officers, wounded at the Battle of Waterloo, recorded in his diary an unsolicited testimonial to its recuperative properties. By the end of the nineteenth century, thirsty travellers were demanding – and were being served – the dark brew in places as far apart as Russia and Havana, Brazil and Turkestan, and had reported their success back to The Brewery, as it is always known in Dublin. Early this century some supplies of Guinness accompanied Scott's expedition to the Antarctic; it was found in a hut at base camp eighteen years later, frozen solid, but otherwise in prime condition.

By the early 1980s, slightly more than eight million glasses of Guinness were being consumed every day in 140 countries around the world, and the advertising slogan 'Guinness is Good for You' had been translated into twenty-two languages, including Chinese and Esperanto. Guinness has breweries in Nigeria and Malaysia as well as the United States and Britain, and it is brewed under licence in South Africa, Australia, New Zealand and Japan; it is particularly popular in Ghana, where the slogan is interpreted as referring to its invigorating effect upon male potency.

Since the early 1980s, consumption has dropped considerably, as part of a world-wide tendency to switch to lighter, lager-type beers; and indeed Guinness now manufacture a very popular lager known as Harp, as well as the most popular of all the alcohol-free lagers, Kaliber. One variety of Guinness, available on draught, used to come in metal containers known in Dublin as 'iron lungs' – hence the familiar, though to tourists baffling call for 'a pint of lung'. Plain porter, a slightly weaker brew, was sold on draught in Ireland only, and the call was always for 'a pint of plain'.

Guinness, however, is not strictly speaking an Irish enterprise, since the Guinnesses, the Earls of Iveagh, are of Anglo-Irish Ascendancy. A current member of the family, however, the Hon. Gareth Browne, is an enthusiast for all matters Celtic; he runs a very successful record company, recording Irish music, called Claddagh Records (Claddagh, after the old fishing quarter in Galway city) and he claims that his ancestors were in

Ireland long before the Norman invasion. Certainly The Product, as employees of The Brewery always call it, is universally recognised as being as distinctively Irish as its logo, the Irish harp. Other versions of the drink are manufactured by Beamish and Murphys, both originating in Cork.

There is no mystique whatever connected with the drinking of Guinness: you simply pour it straight from the bottle or can and knock it back. It can be drunk at room temperature, or slightly chilled, and it goes equally well – or equally badly, according to the view you take of it – with all kinds of food. It is rarely mixed with anything except champagne, to produce a concoction known as Black Velvet, which enjoys a considerable reputation in Ireland both as a hangover cure and as a celebratory libation greatly favoured by the racing fraternity. Mind you, Brendan Behan used to say, and he was probably right, that it wrecked the champagne without doing anything great for the Guinness.

Even the Scots, who sell huge quantities of whisky all over the world, are prepared to concede that it was probably the Irish who invented the drink; the oldest whiskey distillery in the world is Bushmills in County Antrim in Ulster, founded in 1608. You can spell it, by the way, either with or without the 'e'. The Scots and Canadians always omit the 'e'; in Ireland and the States, both spellings are used. Purists argue that there should be an 'e' in the word since it comes from the Gaelic *uisge beatha* (water of life).

Nobody knows when the art of distilling alcohol from a fermented mixture was first discovered – the Greeks knew how to do it in the time of Aristotle – but the Irish were certainly making a cheering spirit from barley when Henry II and his archers arrived in Ireland in the twelfth century. Queen Elizabeth I was partial to a drop of the hard stuff, and Raleigh is known to have picked up a thirty-two-gallon cask for her from the Earl of Cork when he stopped off at Youghal on his way home from one of his voyages.

The Scots, who always had strong connections with France, through the Stuart monarchs and Mary, Queen of Scots, much preferred brandy until the seventeenth century, which may also explain why most Scotch whiskies are blends, and are far closer to brandy both in flavour and in colour than the pale, pure pot-still Irish whiskey. Pot-still gets its name from the copper pot in which it is distilled; it differs from blended whisky in that the final spirit is the result of three distillations from the one original barley mash, and not a blend of several different distillations from several mashes. It is the difference, in a sense, between a vintage and a non-vintage champagne.

That Irish whiskey is not better-known abroad is due to a number of factors. Immediately after the Second World War, there was a world shortage of whiskey. Tillage for barley cultivated for whiskey manufacture was severely curtailed during the war, and there was a shortage of labour in what was quite understandably regarded as a non-priority industry. But whereas the Scotch whisky distillers were ordered to fulfil their export quotas first, and let the home market go short if necessary, the Irish governments of the period, still clinging to the old Sinn Fein self-sufficiency idea, and far more interested anyway in the sure and certain short-term revenue from home sales than in any problematical long-term expansion of export sales, did not encourage Irish distillers to break into the export market.

Another factor undoubtedly is the nature of the spirit itself. Like some of the Scottish straight malts, Irish whiskey is a connoisseur's drink. It does not mix happily with anything other than water (or coffee), and many people accustomed to Scotch or Bourbon find the flavour harsh. Irish whiskey is said not to give you a hangover but I have found from personal experience that this is a fallacy.

A large whiskey is known in Ireland as 'a ball of malt', and is very large: two and a half fluid ounces as against the one ounce and two-thirds of an English 'double'. And a large one is never known as that or as a 'double' in Ireland; on the contrary, the small measure which the Englishman refers to simply as 'a whisky' is usually in Ireland contemptuously called a 'half one'. And it may be significant that the Ulsterman, who paints his letter-boxes an even more assertive shade of red than those in the United Kingdom, sticks to the generous Irish measure when it comes to the seriously important business of dispensing whiskey.

I mentioned coffee above. Many people who find Irish whiskey a little fierce for their taste greatly enjoy it when it is combined with strong black coffee, sugar and thick cream, in the mixture now universally known as Irish Coffee. The secret in making a good Irish Coffee is to heat the glass, and even the whiskey too, if possible; mix the coffee and whiskey, add the sugar and stir until it is dissolved, and then, and only then, when the mixture is sufficiently thickened to support the cream, float a thick layer of double cream very gently over the back of a spoon, so that it lies on the surface of the mixture like the head on a pint of Guinness. It is the effect of drinking the hot, sweet, heady blend of whiskey, coffee and sugar, through the cool, soft, rich cream that gives Irish Coffee its distinctive flavour.

There are numerous accounts of how it came to be discovered and half the bars in San Francisco claim to have invented it, but the plain truth is really very simple. During the Second World War, when VIPs from New York were regularly crossing the Atlantic by flying-boat, via Newfoundland and Foynes in the Shannon estuary, to Lisbon, Portugal, a very bright young man called Brendan O'Reagan was catering manager at Foynes. One night a party asked for *café impériale*, which is a similar drink, but made with cognac. As he had no cognac in stock, Brendan O'Reagan told his staff to try making it with whiskey. It was immediately successful – very largely because the clean, sharp flavour of Irish whiskey bites through the sweet, hot mixture of coffee and cream far more effectively than brandy ever did. Word of its excellence quickly spread all over the United States and soon after the end of the war, Irish Coffee was being served in pubs and clubs and hotels and restaurants all over the world.

The Irish also make a Scotch-type whisky known as Hewitts, and a very agreeable liqueur, rather like the Scottish Drambuie, which has a base of Irish whiskey and honey and is called Irish Mist. A recent success in world markets is Bailey's Irish Cream, a 'traditional' Irish recipe which was invented a few years back by the Irish Milk Marketing Board and the Irish whiskey distillers between them as a profitable means of getting rid of their joint surplus products. It is extremely popular with the ladies, possibly because it looks genteel and bland, but packs quite a deceptive punch.

There's also a new Irish drink called Sheridan's, which comes in a tricky sort of double bottle and, I am told, automatically layers cool vanilla cream liqueur over a rich coffee liqueur, and Carolan's, a third new 'traditional' Irish drink, made from honey, wine and cream. I have not ever felt tempted to try any of them.

The other native Irish drink, *potheen*, roughly corresponds with American moonshine. It is an illicit spirit usually distilled from potatoes in parts of the west and south-west of Ireland. It is a clear spirit, with a flat taste, a sour smell and a kick like slivovitz. I have sampled it on several occasions; one bottle was supplied to me by an ex-policeman who in the course of his career had acquired a good deal of experience of the *potheen* trade and who unhesitatingly recommended it to me as a Château Mouton-Rothschild among *potheens*, but I never found that it had any discernible merit other than an indisputable propensity for making you drunk.

The prevalent English notion that the Irish pubs are open every night and all night is based on a situation that ceased to exist over thirty years ago. Then the pubs opened at about half-past ten in the morning and closed at ten-thirty at night, with an hour's break, known as the Holy Hour, between two-thirty and three-thirty p.m., and that only in the cities, to allow the staff to empty the ash-trays and tidy up a bit. On Sundays, the city pubs opened only between one-thirty and three in the afternoon and again between five and seven o'clock in the evening; the country pubs were not open at all, officially.

The idea behind these extraordinary Sunday opening hours was to enable countrymen, up in Dublin for a Gaelic football or hurling final, to have a drink before the match, and another after it, before setting out on the long voyage home. The effect of this arrangement upon the city drinker was that he often went without both his dinner and his tea on a Sunday, to say nothing about its effects upon the accident rate during the course of the long voyage home for the followers of the sport who lived in the far country.

However, running alongside these strict, puritanical licensing regulations were a whole series of loopholes in the law which made it possible for any determined drinker to pursue his pastime almost right around the clock without breaking the law, or at least without being prosecuted. In Dublin City, during the Holy Hour, all you had to do was to purchase a railway ticket (from Westland Row, say, to Tara Street, just three minutes and a few pence away) and you were entitled, as a voyager, to drink right through the Holy Hour in the buffet on the railway platform. Before the city pubs opened, at ten or half-past ten in the morning, there was always the cattle market, where the pubs opened around half-past five or six, and no questions were ever asked. And after the city pubs closed at ten-thirty, a whole ring of road-houses around the perimeter of the city opened up for what was the main business of their day: the refreshment of bona fide travellers who had journeyed more than five miles away from their home address. No evidence of domicile was ever called for; all you had to do was to be able to think of the name of a suburb more than five miles from the pub, and if you made a mistake and mentioned a suburb inside that limit, the barman more than likely would invite you to have another think, and he'd be back in five minutes.

In the country, on Sundays, the drinking population merely moved from one townland to the next. Around

Knightstown, on Valentia Island, and the Point at Cahirciveen, only about half a mile opposite across the straits that separate – or used to separate before a bridge was built at Portmagee – Valentia from the mainland, or from Ireland, as the islanders always put it, the pubs did a roaring trade with locals who had crossed the water by boat just after mass, and would cross it again in the opposite direction just before bed-time.

This was legal because no one could accurately calculate how long a half-mile journey might take in a rowing boat; and a man prepared to undertake a sea voyage in search of a drink before the bridge was built was obviously a serious traveller of good faith.

Even this procedure was not strictly necessary. There were 'hotels' all over the country where 'residents' who had signed the visitors' book, and their guests, could drink all night. The system reached its absurd apogee in a tiny pub in Avoca in County Wicklow, which had, to everybody's knowledge, only two small bedrooms in which a couple of paying guests were occasionally accommodated. To this pub, every night around closing time, the local sergeant made his ponderous way. Gazing balefully around the bar, which often contained no fewer than fifty people, most of them extremely well known to the sergeant himself, he would address himself to the barman.

'All these good people guests of yours, Victor?' he would ask.

'Oh, yes, Sergeant, each and every one of them stopping under the same roof in this hotel, Sergeant,' Victor would reply.

'Well, if they've all signed the visitors' book,' the sergeant's nightly litany would continue, 'we may as well lock the doors and have a drink or two in peace.'

All has now changed utterly. Since the 1960s, the licensing hours have been extended to eleven-thirty p.m., and it isn't easy to get a barman to take an order much later than a quarter past eleven. On Sundays the pubs stay open until ten-thirty, and are open all afternoon and the bona fide trade has disappeared for ever. And although nothing will convince me that it is not still possible to get a drink in Dublin or anywhere else in Ireland at any time of the day or night, it's certainly a lot harder than it used to be.

On the other hand, Irish drinking habits have changed profoundly, too. The city pubs, particularly the so-called 'singing' pubs, are still doing a roaring trade, but their clients are mainly tourists. Among the Irish yuppies – Tim Pat Coogan's 'mohair brigade' – Ballygowan Spring Water is the smart drink, and it is no longer acceptable to get drunk in public.

'In the part of Dublin I came from,' Brendan Behan once confided to me, 'it was never regarded as a disgrace to get drunk. It was regarded as an achievement.' This is no longer true anywhere in Ireland; drunks in the street have become a rarity, and there is even a Ballygowan School of Irish Writers who believe that mineral water produces far better literature than balls of malt. It remains to be seen. I doubt it.

One reason for all this, of course, may be that in Ireland, as almost everywhere else, the lure of the television screen and the hazards of the drinking and driving laws – recently brought more into line with the rest of the European Union by lowering the permissible limit from 100 milligrams of alcohol to 80 milligrams, and by the imposition of much stiffer penalties including automatic loss of licence for two years and fines of up to £2,000 – have meant, between them, that all the serious drinking in Ireland, like all the serious drinking in France, now takes place in the home, behind closed doors.

12

Irish Inventions, One and All

Sport and Leisure

If the previous chapter gives the impression that the principal leisure-time activity of the Irish is drinking, this, while probably still true, is slightly misleading because it might leave the impression that the Irish are not interested in other sports, which would be completely wrong.

So far from not being interested in other sports, the Irish claim to have invented a great many of them. Among the leisure-time activities embraced by this claim are golf and croquet as well as tennis and cricket, since all stick and ball games are believed (by some of the Irish, at any rate) to have been developed from the ancient Celtic sport of hurling; Rugby football, which is generally thought to have been brought to the English public school of that name by a young West Briton born in County Tipperary, is said to have been based on another ancient Celtic game, Gaelic football; bowls, since a primitive version of road bowling was placed in Ireland centuries before Drake played those famous few ends on the green at Plymouth Hoe before setting forth to defeat the Spanish Armada; and finally, yacht racing.

There could be an element of truth behind all these extravagant claims but they need a bit of sorting out. There is no doubt that a primitive stick and ball game was played in Ireland a very long time ago. There is a reference to the game of hurling in an account of the first Battle of Moytura which is generally believed to have taken place in 1272 BC, long before the final wave of Celts, the magical People of the Danaan, had even arrived in Ireland. And most authorities on the subject seem to agree that the only other serious contenders for the honour of inventing the first game to be played with a stick and a ball include Persia, India, China and Tibet, all of which were in the civilisation business long before Ireland. Interestingly, the name of the game polo comes from the Tibetan *pulu*, meaning willow, the timber used for most polo mallets, as well as for cricket bats.

On the other hand, the Irish can still argue that if they were not the first race in the world to develop a game played with sticks and a ball, they were at least the first race to do it on foot, without the aid and assistance of horses. The warrior hero Cuchulain was a dab hand with a hurley and it is on record in the old manuscripts that he once defended goal single-handed against the united strength of 150 stout opponents. Hurling has been the principal sport of the Celtic Irish through the ages, and records of matches going back to the thirteenth century are in existence. The game was very quickly picked up by the Anglo-Norman invaders who took it back with them to Britain where, the Irish argue, it soon degenerated into the much inferior and far tamer game of hockey.

The pastime of playing hurling was one of the many Irish practices and customs picked up by the Anglo-Norman invaders in the twelfth century which their overlords tried hard to discourage. It was at one period forbidden by law; one of the infamous Statutes of the Kilkenny Parliament of the fourteenth century ordained that 'the commons of the said land of Ireland should quit hurling and apply themselves to the use of the bow and the lance and concentrate on other, gentler games which appertain to arms, whereby the Irish enemies may be better checked by the liege commons in these parts.'

But despite all attempts to proscribe it – or at least confine it to the native peasants now, note, described as the Irish *enemies* – hurling continued to be played in Ireland throughout the entire period of colonisation, and was encouraged by the local overlords who all had their own teams in much the same way that village cricket (another development of the old Celtic game) was encouraged by the squires in England. And it spread throughout the world, the argument runs, in such variegated forms as hockey, cricket, golf, tennis, rounders, baseball, billiards and pelote. There are Irishmen who even claim that polo is merely hurling, played on horseback.

Various forms of football were also popular in ancient Ireland, in some of which the ball was bounced, handled and even carried for short periods. And it is just possible that when William Webb Ellis picked up the ball and carried it towards the goal during a soccer match at Rugby School, he was not trying out a new game which he had just invented, but was subconsciously remembering a Munster version of the Gaelic football he had watched many times as a small boy in County Tipperary. Well, it's possible . . .

And as far as the claim to have invented yacht racing is concerned, one of the oldest yacht clubs in the world, if not the oldest, is the Royal Cork, founded as the Cork Harbour Water Club in 1720 by a group of Anglo-Irish sportsmen. And it could be that the sport of yacht racing developed from the curious, almost naval-style manoeuvres which were the prescribed practice in that club. One of the sailing orders for 1720 ran as follows: 'When the Admiral will have the whole fleet to chase, he will hoist Dutch colours under his flag, and fire a gun from each quarter ... and when he would have chase given over, he will haul in his flag and fire a gun.'

Yacht racing as a sport has for more than a century revolved around one-design class racing – that is to say, races between boats all built to precisely the same design – and there is not much doubt that the first one-design class in the world was the Dublin Bay 'Water Wag'. This fourteen-foot sailing dinghy developed out of an advertisement inserted in the *Irish Times* on 18 September 1886 by a Mr T.B. Middleton.

'It is proposed,' it ran, 'to establish in Kingstown [Dun Laoghaire] a class of Sailing Punts, with centre-boards, all built and rigged the same, so that an even harbour race can be had with a light rowing and generally useful boat.'

In a circular issued around the same time, Mr Middleton puts the case for one-design class racing far more forcibly:

'From a racing point of view, although the fleet will not have the speed of the clippers of the Dublin Bay Sailing Club, yet speed is only found by comparison, and, as all the boats will be the same, a true and most exciting race will ensue, a race where every boat will have the same chance and will call throughout for continued attention in order to gain every little advantage to be got in order to win, and not a mere procession of boats, and a race that will be a contest of the crew and not of designers and sailmakers, a contest also that will be interesting to the shoregoing people as it will be a close one, and the first boat in will be the winner.'

When I first went sailing in Dublin Bay just after the war, I constantly used to encounter an old man called Jones who would sail his Water Wag single-handed around the course, eating oranges and dropping the peel into the water in a very leisurely, laid-back manner. He would watch the fragments of peel as they drifted away, revealing the direction of the eddies in the current at every state of the tide, 'in order to gain every little advantage to be got in order to win', which he usually did, and the Wags were a splendid sight as they fanned out of the harbour mouth towards the Seapoint mark. They still sail in Dublin Bay every Saturday afternoon and Thursday evening during the season.

It used to be widely believed in the United Kingdom that all foreign games were banned in Ireland. This notion arose from a ban imposed by the Gaelic Athletic Association (the body which runs the ancient and exclusively Irish field games of hurling and Gaelic football) upon its members prohibiting them from playing, or even watching, such 'foreign' games as cricket, rugby and hockey. As we have seen, these could not, strictly speaking, be regarded as foreign games since they were all developments of the old Gaelic games, but the ban was primarily introduced to discourage potential Gaelic football players from picking up a fondness for soccer as a result of playing football with units of the British forces stationed in the Curragh and elsewhere in Ireland. However, it later resulted, among other absurdities, in the suspension of Dr Douglas Hyde, one of its own founder-members when, as first President of the Irish State, he attended a Rugby International in Dublin.

The reason for continuing the ban after independence was logical enough; it was to prevent potential hurling and Gaelic football stars from being lured away by the blandishments of 'foreign' games which offered, among other attractions, the highly tempting bait of big money and international fixtures. That is why the ban never applied to the more pukka sports such as golf, hunting, yacht racing or polo; the sort of people who played hurling and Gaelic football were not likely, in those days, to take up golf or polo or yachting. Now the situation has changed completely, and the ban has long since disappeared along with so many other abandoned dreams.

But during the many long years that it existed – from 1886 until the late 1960s – it threatened instant suspension, not merely for any member who played any of the forbidden foreign games, but for any member of the Gaelic Athletic Association who attended a match or even a dance or any other function in any way connected with these games; and it provided an early example of that devious, evasive variety of double-think that is curiously Irish. The ban was administered with the aid of a posse of 'vigilantes' who roamed the rugby pitches, soccer fields and hockey club premises, spying on their fellow-members – they didn't actually attend the rugby club dances, presumably for fear of contamination, but hung around outside, scrutinising the clients as they arrived.

And the existence of this force of vigilantes enabled the Gaelic Athletic Association to find a 'constitutional' way, as Mr de Valera used to put it, out of one of their difficulties: the recalcitrance of some of their top players. If a brilliant Gaelic footballer – who would be a sad loss to the game if he had to be suspended under the association's rules – appeared determined to defy the rules and attend international rugby matches, he would simply be appointed a vigilante. Then, of course, it immediately became his duty to attend the rugby matches he was determined to watch anyway.

As to the games themselves, hurling looks like a cross between a shillelagh fight and a highly dangerous, high-speed form of hockey. The hurley – a stout, unsprung ashplant – is swung around in the air a great deal of the time, and it seems a miracle that broken heads are not a lot commoner than they are. The rules are extremely flexible; I think there is one which declares that it is unlawful to raise the hurley above your head when striking down a player not actually in possession of the ball at the time.

Gaelic football is also very fast; it is played with a round ball, like soccer, but the ball can be bounced and handled as well as kicked on a pitch considerably larger than a football or rugby one, which makes for a faster game. Both games are played with teams of fifteen men a side. Substitutes are allowed and usually required, and the goal posts are similar to rugby ones; in both games goals are scored under the cross-bar and points over it.

Inevitably, the Gaelic games are losing ground to hockey, cricket and rugby, and with Jack Charlton, or Saint Jack as he is known to the Irish, in charge of the Irish international football team, which includes several black players and hardly one true Gael – at least eleven of the players were recruited from English teams – soccer is now the main big box-office attraction. More than 15,000 supporters, including almost the entire Cabinet, followed the Irish football team across the Atlantic to the United States for the World Cup in the summer of 1994, and not a tap of work was done in Dublin until the Irish team were out of the running.

But despite desertions to 'foreign' games like soccer, both by players and followers of the Gaelic games, the old Celtic sports still have a very strong following and capacity attendances at All-Ireland finals at Croke Park are not uncommon. Incidentally, the border is ignored by supporters and players of both Rugby football and the two Gaelic games, as it is indeed by the Church; both the Catholic Church and the Protestant Church of Ireland still have their primacies sited in Saint Patrick's old headquarters at Armagh. The Irish Rugby International team includes players from all over Ireland, and in the days when every alternative 'home' match used to be played in Belfast, the call, from Unionist as well as Republican throats, was always 'Come on, Ireland', and even today, the attendance at rugby international matches in Lansdowne Road, Dublin, always includes a sizeable contingent from Ulster. And when, in 1960, County Down won the All-Ireland Gaelic Football final at Croke Park, the Lord Mayor of Belfast gave a civic reception for the team and their supporters in the City Hall, apparently accepting with good grace the evidence of so many enthusiastic Gaelic Nationalists in one of the six 'loyal' counties.

Another traditional Irish sport which is literally nearing the end of its road is the Irish version of bowls, known as road bowling. The bowlers, usually carrying fairly heavy bets, hurl small iron balls along lonely country roads. Distance is the main object of the exercise, rather than strategic placing as in English bowls and French *pétanque*, and the aim is to cover a certain number of miles in the minimum number of throws. Though Irish roads are still relatively empty by world standards, the opportunities for playing this game in any degree of safety are rapidly disappearing.

Greyhound racing is another sport which, while it may not have originated in Ireland, is certainly nourished from there: ninety per cent of all the dogs racing in the United Kingdom are of Irish ancestry and the Republic is the biggest producer of racing dogs in the world. There is dog racing on most nights in Dublin and there are tracks in many of the towns throughout the country.

Coursing, an older and cruder form of greyhound racing, in which pairs of dogs are set on live hares, is still very popular throughout the country and is sometimes quoted as a sign of the Irish lack of concern for animals. The defenders of coursing argue that the hare stands a sporting chance but this defence is only ever trotted out to silence critics; and although recent regulations have meant that the greyhounds have to be muzzled, this has reduced the amount of blood shed, but has done very little to alleviate the discomfort suffered by the hares. In any event, I doubt if the gentlemen who follow this sport would lose a single night's sleep if all the hares in any meeting were killed, though in practice only about a third of them ever were. This lack of concern for the suffering of animals may stem partly from religion. Throughout history, animals have tended to get pretty short shrift in the most fervent Catholic and Muslim countries. Or it may have something to do with the fact that farmers haven't much time to worry about how animals feel about things, though it also has a lot to do with living standards in general. Lap-dogs are far more common in Dublin today than they were a generation ago, and if the standard of living continues to escalate, they may become as obtrusive and objectionable as they now are all over France. For the moment, at least, good sense prevails in Ireland and in general dogs are kept severely in their place, with a prod of the toe, if necessary, to preserve discipline and obedience.

Other sports, like golf, athletics and cycling, attract about the same sort of support as they get in the other countries of the European Union. But, when any competitor does have a big international success – as, for example, when Stephen Roche from Carrick-on-Suir, County Tipperary, won the Tour de France cycle race in 1987 – it tends to grab an inordinate amount of publicity all over the English-speaking world, probably because so many of the Irish who have emigrated have gone into one or another of the communications industries.

Golf, angling, sea-fishing, shooting and yachting, once strictly reserved for the Ascendancy classes, are now widely and about equally shared by the descendants of Saint Patrick's people and their paying guests from all over the world. In Ireland the rivers are beautiful and underfished and the price of a rod for the day is lower than almost anywhere else in the Western world. Ireland also used to be about the only country in the Western world with so many golf courses in beautiful countryside that there was no need for anybody to queue up. Now the sport has become so popular that the courses are as crowded and the clubs as expensive as they are anywhere else.

Which leaves the horses. The Anglo-Irish were great horse-fanciers and it is largely as a result of their influence that there is racing in Ireland nearly every day of the year on some of the loveliest racecourses you could find anywhere. The famous Dublin Horse Show is another Anglo-Irish promotion; it is run by the Royal Dublin Society, a well-meaning West British organisation established in 1731 'for the purpose of improving husbandry, manufactures and other useful arts and sciences'; it assumed the title 'Royal' in June 1820, when George IV became its patron. The National Stud at Tully, County Kildare, was formerly a private stud, established by an eccentric Englishman, Lord Wavertree, and presented by him to the British Government, who in turn presented it to the Irish Government in 1943. And although the famous Irish packs are now followed by horses carrying Irish Catholic farmers, lawyers, doctors, bankers and businessmen, all of the famous hunts were established by the *Sassenach* (as the Brits used to be called in Ireland).

The myth that the Irish are a great horse-loving people is another legacy of the British rule. The native Irish love something for nothing. Betting shops are far more crowded than race meetings and many of the most ardent racing followers never go near a racecourse. Alan Bestic, in *The Importance of Being Irish* (London: Cassell, 1969) observed an even more curious phenomenon: women who went to the races sat outside the Tote on a little wall, drinking beer from the bar while their children played happily around them. They didn't even watch the races. As one of the husbands remarked: 'God, no! They didn't bother about the races. They just had their drink and their bet and the good fresh air. Wasn't that enough for them?'

The first governments of the Irish Free State were very quick to cotton on to this aspect of the Celtic character. They promoted the Irish Hospitals Sweepstakes to finance the Dublin hospitals which were then in a very bad way, by means of a lottery cunningly disguised to look as if it was actually a development of the old Irish infatuation with horses. The tickets drawn out of the drum by Irish nurses were matched to the names of horses running in all the classic races, and even if you were lucky enough to draw a horse, you didn't know whether or how much you had won until the race had been run. These days, all pretence of any ancient connection with horse-racing has been dropped and the Irish were running a highly successful twice-weekly straight National Lottery long before the British one started in 1994. Some of the proceeds of the lottery go to the arts, heritage, and other good causes as well as the hospitals, but nobody is in any doubt about the main motive of the subscribers: the overweening and fairly universal desire to win a great deal of money.

But the one thousand acres or so of the best horse-breeding country in the world which were bequeathed to the Irish Government by Lord Wavertree, via the British Government, have proved a gold mine. Developed as they have been by one of the Irish semi-state companies, the National Stud has become a top dollar-earner, a useful export industry as well as a continuing advertisement for the country. It is operated largely for the benefit of Irish bloodstock breeders, and to give Irish farmers with brood mares a chance of breeding from the best blood available, a nominal three hundred-guinea (£315) stud-fee is charged (with a no foal, no fee, guarantee) and applicants are chosen by drawing names out of a hat. The

National Stud has occasionally run into trouble; for example when, right at the outset of its activities, it paid what was then the highest price ever for a race horse (£250,000) to the richest man in the world (the Aga Khan) for a stallion called Tulyar, at a time when unemployment had reached 90,000 and the country was in a terrible state of depression. But Tulyar – whose progeny never made any great mark on the racing scene – was sold again at no loss to the country, unemployment has now settled down at close on the 300,000 mark, the sky hasn't fallen in on anybody yet, and the National Stud is still making a respectable profit. Irish horses and trainers are always in the news, especially Vincent O'Brien who, until his retirement a couple of years ago, was the leading figure in Irish racing; his stables are in County Tipperary. He has trained horses which have won three Grand Nationals, three Cheltenham Gold Cups, three Cheltenham Hurdles and the Arc de Triomphe Stakes at Longchamps in Paris, among them Arkle, who was famous not only for all the races he won, but also because he clearly enjoyed his pint of Guinness at the end of a long day.

13

The Failte Industry

Tourism, Festivals and the Pop Scene

I have always believed Ireland's most valuable single resource to be the beauty of the Irish landscape. Even allowing for a slight element of chauvinism, I don't think that it is inaccurate to state that there is no land area anywhere of comparable size – and I am including Northern Ireland in this extravagant claim – which offers such a staggering variety of natural and unspoilt scenery within very easy reach of all the appurtenances of civilisation. Switzerland has the edge where lofty, snow-capped mountain peaks are concerned, but Ireland also has the sea, and although Ireland's mountains are not high (the highest is around one thousand metres), hills everywhere tend to set their own scale and Ireland's, while remaining extremely accessible, generally give an impression of immense grandeur and majesty.

You can put your after-lunch brandy glass (always provided that somebody else is doing the driving) down on the table in the dining room of the Shelbourne Hotel in the centre of Dublin and within half an hour you can be on the top of the Dublin Mountains, in a landscape as remote and deserted as any in Connemara or the Scottish Highlands, without a single dwelling or any other sign of human existence in sight.

Or if you prefer the sea, you can go to An Lar, as the centre of Dublin City is now called, since the famous pillar was blown up from under Nelson's statue in 1966, to commemorate the fiftieth anniversary of the 1916 Easter Rising, and the old city tram and bus terminal, for over a century known as Nelson's Pillar, had to be renamed. From there you can take a bus to Sandymount, and in twenty minutes or so find yourself walking out to meet the tide on Sandymount Strand.

I don't think there is any other capital city in the world capable of offering such a felicitous and convenient access both to the mountains and to the sea.

Again allowing for a slight element of chauvinism, I also think it is true that Ireland's second most valuable resource, in terms of the tourist industry, is the overall and almost overwhelming feeling of welcome which the Irish instantly exude at the approach of a stranger from any shore, even the British one. It's not something Saint Patrick's people can take any great credit for: they can't help it, it's in their very nature. It would be very convenient and handy if one could simply put it down to the fact that they happen to be Celts, but there's no way that any stranger ever feels as welcome in Brittany or Wales as everybody does in Ireland. The Irish at home seem to be on a permanent party. Years ago, when Ronnie Delaney won a Gold Medal at the Olympic Games in Melbourne, Australia, for running 1,000 metres in three minutes and 41.2 seconds on 2 December 1956, he was subsequently offered a place in a sports-orientated university in the United States, and his father visited him there. On his return the old man reported to his local bowling club, Railway Union, that America was all right, except that everybody seemed to work like mad for the rest of the year, so that they could enjoy a couple of weeks vacation in the summer. 'That wouldn't suit me at all,' he added. 'Over here in Ireland we're on holiday the whole year round.' Maybe that's the secret; certainly if you stop your car and ask an Irishman the way to some place, he's as likely as not to get into the car and accompany you there, and if you give him the slightest encouragement, he'll spend the rest of the day with you, and pay for half the drinks into the bargain.

Whatever it is that makes Ireland an attractive tourist centre, it was very quickly recognised by the early governments of the Irish Free State. In the 1920s they set up an Irish Tourist Association of hoteliers and *restaurateurs*, though not many people wanted to visit Ireland in the immediate aftermath of the Troubles if they could possibly help it, and for obvious reasons. After the war, the government had a rethink and set up a state-sponsored body to encourage and control tourism. They conceived the bright idea of calling it An Bord Failte (the Welcome Board) and extending the scope of its activities to include pubs and bed-and-breakfast accommodation, racecourses and dog-tracks, firms producing picture post-cards, railway timetables and tourist literature and indeed each and everyone conceivably connected with the welcome business in Ireland.

As it happened, the Irish Welcome Board got off to a bad start. Initially inspired, perhaps, by a desire to attract back to Ireland some of the GIs who had been stationed in Northern Ireland during the Second World War, and who fondly remembered excursions south of the border in the course of which they discovered a great place for big steaks, bright lights and good conversation, the Irish tourist authorities began by trying to attract those ex-servicemen, and their wives and families, to return and re-live their heightened memories of a land of peace and plenty.

Unfortunately it just didn't work. The trouble was that in the period immediately following the war, things were bad in Ireland; in some ways the austerity we suffered was far more severe even than that in England. True, there was no real shortage of food, but there wasn't much variety and there were other, far more serious, shortages for a country trying to attract American tourists.

There was almost no fuel, apart from turf. Hotels were cold and damp, and hot water was scarce. Shortages of bed-linen and crockery, furnishings and fittings gave some hoteliers an excuse for the execrable service they would probably have provided anyway. The trains ran, or failed to run, on turf and wood, with the result that journeys which should have taken a couple of hours sometimes lasted from early morning until late at night. The coaches were unheated and the trains frequently stopped for hours at a time, miles away from anywhere, while the engineers were trying to coax a head of steam from the reluctant turf. And on top of all of this, prices were ridiculously high: sensing that they would probably never see this lot again, the Irish hoteliers, restaurant owners and taxi-drivers did their best to fleece them while the going was still fairly good.

The ex-servicemen were succeeded by another equally disastrous wave of tourists, who were all wrong for what the country then had to offer. They were mainly lower-middle or working-class families from the Midlands and Lancashire who were attracted to Ireland by tales then being told of cheap beer and tobacco and large, juicy steaks; the sort of people accustomed to spending their holidays in places like New Brighton and Blackpool, where there is plenty to do in the form of fish and chip shops, amusement arcades, pier-head variety shows, and trips around the bay on the *Nancy Belle*. Ireland is mercifully short on such amenities, and it is no wonder that those who brought their teenage children with them to Ireland in the immediate post-war period had to put up with their offspring's complaints that there was nothing to do; no plentiful supply, in other words, of young people of their own age with whom they could form holiday attachments of one sort or another, or rather, no places in which it was feasible to meet them. Like the ex-servicemen from the United States, they went back home vowing that they would never set foot in the place again.

A fresh drive for tourists began in 1957, and it soon became apparent, from the sort of advertisements that were then being placed and the type of newspapers and magazines that they were being placed in, that Ireland was setting out to attract a new and better-heeled type of customer.

In the years immediately after the war, most of the Irish hotels had been improved and enlarged with the aid of government grants and loans. New wings were added with private bathrooms and other 'American comforts', as they were then termed, staff were properly trained, and tourist offices were opened in Britain, North America and all over the European continent. The Irish Tourist Board would never have admitted that it was catering mainly for the better-heeled tourists and indeed its officials could even point to the fact that they had also been shelling out good money for improvements to cheaper accommodation such as the excellent 'bed and breakfast' facilities then and still available in Ireland. But it is a fact that in the 1960s and 1970s, Ireland appealed to the more prosperous tourist, who would be attracted by its scenery, its peace, its pace, by the amenities it offered in the way of such sports as golf, shooting, yachting and fishing, and who would be far less likely to be put off by the bad weather.

A sudden downpour is not likely to spoil your holiday if you have brought over your own Rover, or hired a Mercedes, but it can prove pretty disastrous if you are trying to picnic on the wet grass five miles or so away from the Enniskerry bus stop, with only a plastic mackintosh for shelter. Ireland is now succumbing to the generally-accepted Northern European practice of providing weather-insulated holiday complexes with large swimming pools in controlled-temperature plastic bubbles like the Centerparcs in England.

Aware of the need to do something more dynamic to establish Ireland on the international scene as a major tourist attraction, the 1953 Welcome Board came up with the notion of An Tostal. The words simply mean 'the pageant', though initially the Tostal had no pageant whatever connected with it; in fact it consisted of nothing more than would have been on offer anyway in the theatres, restaurants, hotels and pubs in Dublin and throughout the country. If it was supposed to commemorate anything, the Irish Tourist Board, who dreamed up the idea, never let anybody in on the secret of what it was. One of its stated aims was to attract the Irish overseas to return to Ireland for their holidays.

The only concession the Government made to commemorate the occasion was the provision of a 'Bowl of Light' (a vulgar concoction of concrete and Perspex with an electric version of the everlasting flame that endlessly flickers under the Arc de Triomphe in Paris to commemorate the dead of two world wars) on O'Connell Bridge. It was widely known in Dublin as 'The Thing', though *Irish Times* columnist Myles na gCopaleen always referred to it as 'The Tomb of the Unknown Gurrier', and it was quickly and very properly uprooted from its moorings and flung into the River Liffey by discerning architectural and engineering students of University College, Dublin.

But although the Tostal eventually acquired an annual and disastrous pageant, usually based on some legend connected with Saint Patrick or Cuchulain or one of the other heroes of Irish antiquity – usually disastrous because the Irish share none of their next-door neighbour's flair for pomp and circumstance – the idea of festivals as a means of attracting tourists lived on and today they are an integral part of the Irish life style, and attract more foreign tourists than Irish emigrants.

One of the first and still one of the most successful was the Wexford Festival of Grand Opera, which began in 1951 before the first Tostal and may indeed have been its inspiration. From its inception, when the tiny Victorian Theatre Royal was reconstructed – and since there was no room for an orchestra pit in front of the stage, accommodation to house a full-size opera orchestra was built under the stage – the Wexford Festival has always concentrated on little-known operas by well-known composers, and one of its most attractive features was the fact that the whole town went *en fête* for the fortnight of the festival.

The music is probably better at Glyndebourne, but music is all you get at Glyndebourne. In Wexford, because the place is so small, and because the opera singers and conductors all stay at the same two or three big hotels, you keep running into them. You see them enjoying their breakfast in White's Hotel, or having dinner after the show in the Talbot. And every October the Irish sense of time, never very strong, completely deserts them in Wexford, so that if you ever do succeed in getting an early night, and slip into one of the hotels around eleven o'clock in the morning for a coffee, you are quite likely to run into a party still in evening dress, and still on the champagne. There is nothing quite like it anywhere else in the world.

These days, though, the Wexford Festival is only one of many. Whatever time of the year you choose to visit Ireland, you can be pretty certain to run into a festival of one sort or another. There's the Waterford International Festival of Light Opera in September (when the streets are full of Welsh tenors singing and drinking) and the Galway Oyster Festival at Clarenbridge in the same month to mark the opening of the oyster season; the O'Carolan Harp Festival in Keadue, County Roscommon, in August, in the former home of Ireland's great seventeenth-century blind harpist, Turlough O'Carolan; the Kenmare Walking Festival in June; a Match-Making Festival at Lisdoonvarna, County Clare, in September and Puck Fair at Killorglin, in County Kerry, in August.

Puck Fair is a curious business. Part horse fair, part carnival, it attracts the tinkers (as the travelling people used to be called in Ireland; they are now known as travellers, as they are in Britain and many other places) from miles around, and incorporates an ancient pagan rite which may well go back to the days before Saint Patrick's arrival in Ireland. The highlight of the event is the crowning of a billy-goat as King Puck; the unfortunate animal is enthroned and then hoisted to the top of a tall tower of tubular steel scaffolding, where he remains tethered for the three days of the fair, known as Gathering, Puck and Scattering. In the old days, the goat was probably ritually sacrificed to one or other of the old Celtic gods or goddesses at the conclusion of the festivities, but these days he is permitted to rejoin the herd and resume his former activities. And there's the *Fleadh Ceoil* (literally feast, or banquet of music), or rather the *Fleadhanna* (the plural of *fleadh*) *Ceoil*, a travelling jamboree of traditional song and dance and drink that seems to go on all the time, and all over the place.

In some ways the most successful festival of them all is that of the Rose of Tralee, a competition now in its thirty-seventh year and still going strong. For the past twenty or twenty-five years it has been televised by RTE, Ireland's radio and television network, over two successive nights, with Gay Byrne interviewing some thirty or thirty-five beauties from all over the world who aspire to the title of the Rose of Tralee, a lady immortalised in one of Tom Moore's verses, set to an ancient Irish melody. The rules and regulations of the contest are extremely flexible: the prospective rose must be able to claim an Irish parent, grandparent, or great-grandparent, or some connection, however tenuous, with the ould sod, an arrangement which enables the finals of the contest to take place between a San Francisco Rose, a Sydney Harbour Rose and a couple of Roses from Germany and one from

Tokyo, as well as the usual complement of Irish ones.

And while they cannot strictly be classified as festivals, though they often turn into something of the sort, there are all the literary get-togethers, like the James Joyce Summer School in Dublin every July, the Listowel Writers' Week in County Kerry in June and the Kiltartan Hedge School at Gort, County Galway, in July, devoted to the Ballylee writings of W.B. Yeats, as well as half a dozen others, including the annual Bloomsday Walk, when parties of Joyce enthusiasts re-trace the footsteps of Stephen Dedalus, Buck Mulligan, Leopold and Molly Bloom and Blazes Boylan and all the rest of Joyce's splendid cast of characters as they criss-crossed Dublin and its environs on that original Bloomsday, 16 June 1904.

The first of these summer schools was the Merriman Summer School, held in County Clare, usually Lahinch or Kilkee, in August. It was also the first of the summer schools to elect to hold a second session, to brighten up the long winter days with a weekend of drinking, talking and occasional lectures. Those who attend these schools are known, naturally enough, as the merrymen.

Before the Second World War, there was only one festival, if you could even have called it that: Dublin's annual *Feis Ceoil* (literally feast of music), a fortnight of competitions for performers on all instruments as well as a major contest for singers. In its time it has launched quite a few operatic stars, including John MacCormack and Margaret Burke Sheridan, on their international careers. This particular feast of music was largely based on and planned around the sort of singing and performing in the home which was so much a part of the Dublin

Victorian domestic scene: party pieces on the violin or melodeon and songs accompanied by the piano. There was nothing particularly Irish about it, apart from the nationality of the participants; most of the test pieces came from the standard classic repertoire of the period, though the singers usually included a few songs by Percy French or Thomas Moore in their recitals.

If Ireland until the 1930s and 1940s could claim to have made any mark upon the musical map of the world it would have been in terms of mainstream European classical music. For instance John Field, an Irishman, pioneered the 'nocturne' form which Chopin perfected, and the first performance of Handel's *Messiah* was held in Dublin in 1742; indeed both Handel and Thomas Arne (1710–78), the leading English composer of his day, had lived for a time in Dublin. Two Irish grand operas, Michael Balfe's *The Bohemian Girl* and Vincent Wallace's *Maritana*, appeared on most English operatic repertoires and symphony music by Irish composers like Charles Stanford and Hamilton Harty used fragments of Irish folk tunes and what were widely regarded as Irish-type harmonies in their compositions.

Yet today, the Irish are famous for a totally new brand of music: a special sort of rock, which incorporates it is said, though who could possibly know, a great deal of the ancient Celtic mysticism. This music is sufficiently strange and exciting to attract a whole generation of young back-packers to Ireland from all over the world, and to result in a situation in which the moment you mention that you are Irish, anywhere, you are immediately bombarded by any young people present with questions about Bob Geldof, U2, The Chieftains, Clannaid, Enya and The Dubliners, as well as Sineid

O'Connor and, more recently, The Cranberries. In Japan, to take one example – where there is a branch of *Comhaltas Ceoltoiri Eireann*, the traditional Irish music movement – young people who never even heard of the ancient Celts are now discovering strains in their own pop musical heritage which hark back to prehistoric times in ancient Erin. It is worth taking a look at how this extraordinary situation has come about.

Such traditional Irish music as had survived from the music of the ancient Celts – again purely orally, since for some reason, unlike the myths and legends, none of it was ever written down by the early Christian scribes and clerics – took the form of the hornpipes, reels and jigs that were played at what were then known as *ceilidhe* (now with the new spelling simplified to *ceili*), indoor versions of the cross-roads set dances which were always a part of the Irish tradition. Another ancient Celtic musical tradition survived in the slow airs, the songs of love and war, sung in a style known as an Sean Nos (literally, the old manner). But these were very rarely heard outside Ireland.

From the late 1930s ballroom dancing became extremely popular in the towns and cities with all classes of the community. Indeed, ballrooms and dance halls remained the standard, accepted meeting place for young Irish men and women on the look-out for partners for temporary or more longterm liaisons until well into the 1960s and 1970s. And most ballroom dances, even in Dublin, and even those organised by what might be loosely described as West British outfits like the Protestant schools' past pupils' associations, included at least a couple of Irish set dances (*The Walls of Limerick* and *The Siege of Ennis* were two favourites) in the evening's programme. They were regarded as 'a bit of gas', and were danced boisterously, though not very expertly since I don't think anybody in those days took Irish music or dancing very seriously. Not even the most ardent Gaels, who took all other aspects of the old Celtic culture very seriously indeed.

Perhaps because the arrival of radio – and particularly Radio Luxembourg – had spread a taste for what used to be called 'dance music', the craze for ballroom dancing spread rapidly throughout the country in the 1940s and 1950s and by the 1960s Irish ballrooms, as they were known, had become enormously successful. They cropped up everywhere – in the cities and towns, on the outskirts of villages, even in the heart of the countryside. In the far west of Ireland, ballrooms similar to that featured in William Trevor's television play *The Ballroom of Romance* were being built; they were no more than vast warehouses of bare concrete. Not much in the way of decor was needed, since the clients danced in near-darkness under multi-coloured, flickering spotlights; all that was required were four walls and a roof plus a band with a strong beat and a sprung floor capable of supporting two or three thousand dancing feet.

These ballrooms spawned two new developments, the show band, and the fill-in beat group. The show bands played mainly their own versions of the musical numbers that currently were being featured in the Top Thirty in the British charts, but they did far more than just play music for dancing; they provided a complete evening's musical entertainment. They had names like The Dreams Showband, The Royal Showband, The Clipper Carlton and The Miami Showband. The hard core of the show band consisted of about eight to ten extremely professional, highly-paid musicians with natty uniforms and set routines. Most of them also had a couple, or a trio, or even a team of dancing girls, and a few solo performers on the Tom Jones role model. They played six or seven nights a week, fifty-two weeks a year, and most of them made a fortune.

In general, the ballrooms opened around nine o'clock and the female clients started to drift in from about half-past nine, but since the male customers never turned up until after the pubs closed, the serious business of the evening rarely got under way much before midnight. To give themselves a bit of a rest and to keep themselves fresh for the heavy-duty dancing, which would take place between midnight and about three o'clock in the morning, the more successful show bands got into the habit of employing beat groups of two or three instrumentalists, possibly with a singer, to warm up the place and entertain the ladies until the menfolk – and the show band itself – arrived. Many of these beat groups performed numbers of their own composition, and most of the instrumentalists played several instruments and sang as well. Because the music was primarily for listening and not for dancing, these beat groups did not have to bother about strict tempo and could experiment with all sorts of adventurous rhythms and effects.

In the meantime, the advent of the *Fleadh Ceoil* in the 1960s (and as many as forty five *fleadhanna* or traditional music festivals might be held in any one year, all in different locations) gave the older rural-based musical traditions access to the streets, halls and pubs of the new young Ireland that was emerging at that period in the wake of the economic boom. The formation in 1951 of *Comhaltas Ceoltoiri Eireann* (literally, the followers of the musicians of Ireland), a movement founded by a group of Irish musicians alarmed by the growing popularity of the show bands and the threat they presented to traditional Irish music, had already given the stamp of authority to the drive to revive Irish traditional music. This group had pledged itself to its restoration and development and had begun to organise festivals and music classes all over the country. In effect, what they did was to go out and rediscover and rescue the ancient Irish musical tradition and create a revival of interest in it which soon escalated away out of their control, and which has since become one of the most distinctive folk-based forms of popular music in the world.

In his book *Ireland and the Irish* (London: Hamish Hamilton, 1994) John Ardagh writes: 'Any listener to the music-making must sense that the Irish personality expresses itself through its music in a very special way. Some experts have referred to a mysterious, even spiritual, quality in Irish traditional music, as if it were reflecting the collective experience of griefs and passions reaching far back into history. Certainly no other country in Europe has retained so rich and vigorous a tradition of this kind of music, orally transmitted and often performed by amateurs. The reasons may lie in history. One nationalist suggested to me that classical music never caught on widely in Ireland because it was an import of the colonisers; and whereas in other countries much of the folk music was later subsumed by classical music and thus distorted, in Ireland it was outlawed by the British after the sixteenth century and forced to go underground. This helped it to keep its purity. Like Irish Catholicism, it became a cherished expression of national identity.'

Other authors have offered other explanations. In

Bringing it All Back Home (London: BBC Publications, 1991), a book which accompanied a BBC TV series on the revival of traditional Irish music, Nuala O'Connor argues that the post-Famine Irish emigrants brought their music across the Atlantic with them, spawning both a flourishing fad in New York's tin-pan alley pop industry (with hits like 'Mother Machree' and 'If You're Irish, Come into the Parlour') and what became at least a part of the great revival of American Country and Western music in the 1950s and 1960s. There was the specific case of the Clancy Brothers who emigrated from Tipperary in 1947, formed themselves into a popular folk-group in New York in the 1950s and then returned to Ireland to give a series of concert tours in 1961 which served to awaken the interest of many young Irish instrumentalists in the possibilities of their own traditional music. The Clancy Brothers are said to have been greatly influenced by Pete Seeger, and are themselves widely believed to have influenced Bob Dylan, but popular music is full of cross-fertilisations of all kinds.

Ireland's re-discovery of its ancient music coincided with the industrial boom of the late 1960s and culminated in Sean O'Riada's attempt to form a band of traditional musicians of the highest calibre, *Ceoltoiri Cualann* (musicians of Cuala, another ancient name for Ireland).

Sean O'Riada, who did more than any single person to revitalise Irish traditional music during his very short lifetime (1931–71), was a jazz pianist, a composer, and Professor of Music at University College, Cork. Although his *Ceoltoiri Cualann* fell far short of his hopes for it, it did result in the formation of The Chieftains, a group whose uncompromising arrangements of traditional Irish music and use of traditional Irish instruments made them an instant success; their records topped the charts again and again and they toured the world, including China. They used traditional instruments such as the *bodhran*, a goat-skin drum which is beaten with the fist, or played with a small drumstick, and the *uillean* (elbow) pipes, which have a very different sound from the Scottish pipes, as well as more familiar traditional instruments like the concertina, the harp, the fiddle and the tin-whistle. They were followed into the charts by other groups like The Dubliners.

Influenced by the success of The Chieftains and The Dubliners, as well as by The Beatles and The Rolling Stones in Britain, Irish pop groups started springing up all over Ireland, but particularly in Dublin and Belfast where they performed nightly in clubs and cellars. To make money, some of them worked as fill-in beat groups for the show bands for part of the time; and conversely, some of the beat groups who had worked full-time as a fill-in for the show bands began to break away and run their own gigs in the Dublin cellar clubs using a curious new blend of electric guitar and violin with traditional Irish rhythms and even mixing them with traditional Irish and other acoustic instruments.

Mark J. Prendergast charts the developments of those days in *Irish Rock* (Dublin: O'Brien Press, 1987). One of the first groups to emerge from the Dublin cellar clubs with an album recorded by Decca was Thin Lizzy in 1971, and it is significant of the whole Irish rock movement that the lyrics of the first track, 'The Friendly Ranger at Clontarf Castle', drew for its inspiration on ancient legend and history:

In the land of Eireann
Where sat the high king
Faced with a problem
Dreaded Viking
Gather all the menfolk
Speaking the Celtic tongue
The land is Eireann
The land is young

Other Irish groups of the period included Horslips, Peggy's Leg, Granny's Intentions, Eyeless and Dr Strangely Strange. In one number by the latter group there is a curious cross-reference both to the menace to traditional Irish music represented by the show bands, and to one aspect of nationalism:

The mighty cretin show band
Lead the pikemen from the rear
And nobody sees the unicorn
Quietly standing there

The Horslips were approached by the Abbey Theatre in 1972 to provide music for an adaptation of the *Tain Bo Cuailgne*, mentioned in Chapter Two; the album sleeve-notes carried a quotation from W. B. Yeats: 'We Irish should keep these personages much in our hearts, for they lived in the places where we ride and go marketing, and sometimes they have met one another on the hills that cast their shadows upon our doors at evening.'

The album was such a success on the world rock scene that the group did a world tour and played to huge audiences all over the States and Canada. In 1976 they followed this up with an attempt to set to music the twelfth-century chronicle, *The Book of Invasions*, which records all the pre-Christian conquests of Ireland, a highly ambitious undertaking which was highly successful artistically as well as commercially.

Then in 1970, in Gweedore, County Donegal, four members of the same family formed the group known as *Clannad*, using lyrics in Irish and freely mixing folk, jazz and classical styles. In 1973 they produced an album called *Clannad* which featured the distinctive singing and harp-playing of Maire Ni Bhraonain, one of the four members of the Brennan family in the group. Another member of the same family who joined *Clannad* later was Maire's youngest sister, Eithne Ni Bhraonain, who later broke away from the group and changed her name to Enya. Both wrote incidental music for films, Clannad for the television film *Harry's Game*, and Enya for the English film producer David Puttnam's film, *The Frog Prince*.

From its first beginnings, the Irish rock scene ignored the border, just as both main branches of the Christian Church and the Rugby Football Union had always done. Dublin groups frequently did gigs in the Belfast clubs and cellars and vice versa; and Van Morrison, who appeared with Bob Dylan at a historic rock concert at Slane Castle in 1984, was born in Belfast. And when eventually the ballrooms disappeared, to be replaced by discos, a surprisingly high percentage of the pop records picked by the disc jockeys turned out to have been recorded by Irish groups.

And although the group U2, with Larry Mullet, David Evans (The Edge), Paul Hewson (Bono) and Adam Clayton, created Irish rock history by making the cover of the news magazine *Time* in April 1987, they were at the time, and have since remained, one of the most popular and successful rock groups in the world. Bob Geldof is probably better known on the world scene for his highly successful promotion of the Live-Aid concerts and the Band-Aid disc, 'Do They Know It's Christmas', which he organised to raise funds for the famine in Ethiopia. Bob Geldof is an extremely articulate and likeable personality – at one of The Boomtown Rats' concerts at Finsbury Park in London, he yelled, at the end of his own set: 'It doesn't matter a fuck whether you clap or not, we're coming back for an encore anyway.' Of course, he had the added advantage, from a publicity point of view, of being married to the outspoken and unpredictable British rock personality, Paula Yates.

And in the meantime, ever since a gap-toothed girl from Derry, Rosemary Brown, who was better known as Dana, won the Eurovision Song Contest for Ireland in 1970, the Irish have won it more consistently than any other nation, ending up by winning it for three years running, in 1991, 1992 and 1993.

The 1993 contest was given an extremely lavish production at Dublin's new concert hall, the Point, a converted warehouse on the quays right beside the new toll bridge, and it featured Bill Whelan's *Riverdance*, a spectacular revival of another ancient Irish art form, traditional Irish dancing. Two Irish-Americans (Joan Butler, who went to both Irish dancing and ballet classes as a child in New York and who managed to fuse the two in a dazzling display of feather-light flashing feet, and her partner, Michael Flatley) were the stars of a company that has put Irish dancing very firmly on the international map both with their performance at the 1993 Eurovision Song Contest and again when they headed the bill at the Royal

Variety Command Performance in December 1994 and during subsequent performances all over the world. What made their performance so magical was the total transformation of the dreary ceilidhe/crossroads style of dancing, in which pale, solemn, downcast girls and shy lads wearing Pioneer (Total Abstinence Society) badges used to bounce up and down joylessly with their arms held stiffly down by their sides, into this exuberant, pagan, loin-stirring extravaganza. It uses all the magic of current state-of-the-art sound recording to turn the timid heel-tapping of the step-dancers of yore into a thunderous roar with all the urgency of a flamenco coming straight out of Spain, or something even more primitive and primeval. The British producer Cameron Mackintosh called it '... one of the most exciting mixtures of folk dance and music combined with Broadway pizzaz I have ever seen ... completely thrilling.'

Yet another score to be marked up for the successors of Saint Patrick's people.

14

Far from the Land

The Irish Abroad

The Irish are a perverse people, full of contradictions. There is, for example, the fact that, in relation to their population, they have probably produced a far higher proportion of playwrights and poets, novelists and writers of all kinds than any other nation. Yet as a race, they did not even begin to learn to read and write until long after the Hebrews had assembled all their historical records and rules and regulations and myths and legends, into the book that we now know as the Old Testament, nor until long after both the Talmud and the Koran, as well as the New Testament, had been dictated and transcribed and the whole corpus of Greek and Roman literature had been composed, collected, copied out and distributed through the libraries of the ancient world.

Then there is the curious fact that although Great Britain and Ireland lie between roughly the same degrees of latitude and longitude and enjoy, if that's the word for it, the same sort of damp, cold climate, in Britain these conditions have turned the descendants of the Romans,

Danes, Anglo-Saxons and Anglo-Normans into a race of serious, hard-working, law-abiding citizens who unwind only very reluctantly, whereas in Ireland, the descendants of the Celts – mixed with Danish, Norman, Scots, Anglo-Saxon and other strains – have managed to remain as laid back and as easy-going, in many ways, as the peoples who live on the Mediterranean littoral.

The English always seem to be in a hurry while, at the drop of a hat, the Irish will still insist on telling all those time-worn, clichéd jokes about themselves in order to emphasise and underline the huge differences between the two adjoining nations. For instance, in Ireland you are constantly and confidently assured that when God made time, he made plenty of it, and that the Irish share with the Spanish people the basic concept of *mañana*, with the added difference that in Ireland it doesn't have anything like the same sense of urgency.

Even more perverse and paradoxical, perhaps, is the Irish attitude towards their own native land. No people in the world are so fiercely proud as the Irish are of their homeland, or as deeply and sentimentally moved by the beauty of its landscape, of the mountains and hills, forests and rills. Indeed, they never tire of singing its praises and of recounting its felicities, mostly in saloons and bars and pubs and clubs in cities and towns situated on the far side of the globe, or at the very least, on the other side of the Irish Sea.

All over the world, and long before Irish rock music made its impact on young people everywhere, Ireland was far better known for its people than for the place itself. Millions of people who have never been to Ireland, and are never likely to go there, know quite a lot about the country. This is because, over the centuries, one of

Ireland's principal exports has been its people, usually the youngest, the most ambitious, and the adventurous ones. And wherever they have gone, the Irish have talked incessantly about the land they left behind them.

The tendency of the Irish to go abroad to live and work reached epidemic proportions in the middle of the nineteenth century, during and immediately after the Great Famine. But what started as a desperate solution to a desperate situation became part of the Irish way of life; and for more than a century after the Famine the Irish continued to rear large families (six or seven children were common and ten or twelve not unusual) in the sure and certain knowledge that they would be forced to emigrate in order to survive.

From the earliest Christian missionaries to the Wild Geese (Irishmen who emigrated to serve as mercenaries in Europe's constantly warring armies), from the huddled masses who in the years following the Great Famine in the middle of the nineteenth century fled Ireland for Ellis Island and its hinterland to the tens of thousands of young men and women unable to earn a living in Ireland who took the easy way out – the mailboat to Holyhead, or the B and I to Liverpool – and found jobs as a barmen or barmaids, nurses, shop assistants or factory workers in England in this century, the Irish have always been forced to go abroad to find a future, and have taken with them the ineradicable stamp of the old country.

Some of the Wild Geese became famous generals: the Avenue MacMahon in Paris is named after one of them. Others went into the wine business. Lynch-Bages is one of Bordeaux's great clarets and the Lynch part of the name is Irish. So is Garvey, one of the best-known of the

Spanish sherries, and Hennessy, one of the most famous of the French cognac brandies.

Many of those who emigrated to the New World prospered too. Everybody knows about the Irish connections of John F. Kennedy and Ronald Reagan, but no fewer than ten other American Presidents also descended from Irish families, including Ulysses Simpson Grant, the Federal Commander in the Civil War, William McKinley and Woodrow Wilson. James Dunlap, who printed the Declaration of Independence, is said to have learned his trade at Gray's printing shop in Strabane, in County Tyrone; Commandant John Barry, who founded the American Navy, came from Wexford; Ambrose O'Higgins emigrated from Daingean, County Meath, to South America, where he became Viceroy of Peru, and where his son Bernardo, a friend of José de San Martin and Simon Bolivar, became Chile's first dictator. Another Irishman, William Brown from Foxford, County Mayo, was one of the founders of the Argentinian Navy.

But for every one of the emigrants who found fame abroad, hundreds of thousands emigrated to an obscurity not greatly different from that which had surrounded them and their ancestors in the old country. They did well, by Irish standards, well enough to revisit, after only a few short years in exile, what they called the ould sod, and to distribute a few dollops of largesse among their admiring friends and relatives, before returning to the ghettoes where they lived in their adopted countries. There, they were only able to slough off their status as second-class citizens by meeting fellow exiles in societies like the Fenians and the Ancient Order of Hibernians and the Irish clubs; by posting back 'remittance' money as it was called, to those of their relatives unlucky enough not to have been able to get their hands on sufficient cash to buy a ticket out of Ireland; and by contributing very lavishly (and, I feel, very foolishly) to funds like Noraid, ostensibly dedicated to the cause of getting the British out of Ireland once and for all, though I have yet to hear a convincing explanation of how blowing up a few Christmas shoppers in a random bomb explosion in Knightsbridge, London, advances the cause of Irish freedom in any way. I have heard Michael Collins quoted as a justification for such acts of terrorism, and it is true that Collins did (or, more accurately, ordered others to do) some dreadful things. But Collins and the Irish Republican Army of 1920 had taken on the British forces of law and order, and they knew that the only way they could win was by provoking them into replying in kind and by meeting atrocity with atrocity, in the sure and certain knowledge that a powerful nation like Britain would never be forgiven by world opinion for resorting to such measures. They also knew that they were putting their own lives on the line. It doesn't seem to me to take very much in the way of courage to plant a brief-case containing, among other things, a few pounds of Semtex in a litter-bin in a crowded shopping mall.

The Irish abroad lived mostly in ghettoes. In London, they lived in a series of what, for want of a better word, might be called 'centres', districts such as Kilburn, Camden Town and Islington, all about equally spaced out in an arc around Euston Station, and about as far away from it as a healthy man could comfortably walk burdened down with the weight of a heavy suit-case. In New York and Nottingham, as well as in Buenos Aires and Boston, there were similar Irish 'centres' where displaced Celts congregated to cheer each other up and to collaborate in charades vaguely based on the old myths and legends.

It was in the United States that the Irish abroad made by far their greatest impact. The destinies of Ireland and the United States are inextricably mixed. The Irish played a prominent part in the American War of Independence, and the Yankee victory in the Civil War was due, in part at least, to the Irishmen of the Fighting 69th.

With the exception of what the Americans call the Scotch-Irish – the 200,000 or so disaffected Scottish non-Conformists who were just as harshly oppressed by the government, under the stern influence of the Established Church of England, and even more severely hit by the economic measures which the British Parliament imposed on Ireland to eliminate Irish competition, because they had far more to lose – the Irish who went to America were mostly peasants, small farmers and cottagers. Yet they congregated in the cities and towns along the eastern seaboard of the United States and made no effort to reach farming country or to look for work on the land.

There were several reasons for this. Most of them had only been able to scrape together the bare passage-money and, like the London Irish who arrived at Euston Station, they could not afford to travel very far away from the port in which their ship docked. In any event, they were not really farmers, but farm labourers. They knew how to dig, but that was the extent of their knowledge of agriculture. And it was small wonder that they had no feeling for the land, which had brought them only misery at home. If the Industrial Revolution had spread to southern Ireland and had resulted in the setting up of big factories in small towns, as it did in England, the Irish peasants would have flocked to them in search of work. Many of them did emigrate to England to work in the factories there; but because Ireland and England belonged at that time to the same kingdom, there is no record of the numbers. The Irish who emigrated to America found plenty of opportunities for men willing and able to use their hands, without venturing any further afield from the towns and cities.

They set to it, digging trenches, making roads, working on building sites. The Erie Canal, linking New York with the Great Lakes, was largely built with Irish labour; so were the 30,000 miles of railroad laid between 1830 and 1860. The female Irish emigrants mostly went into domestic service where, despite a double prejudice against them both as Irish and as Catholics, they were in great demand because in the main they could be trusted not to steal and tended not to cause too much trouble by undue dallying with the menfolk of the household.

The Irish emigrants, when they first arrived in America, seemed completely content to live in slums and hovels, in overcrowded conditions which horrified the older-established American settlers. What the latter didn't realise, perhaps, was that these slums and ghettoes, ghastly as they were, were a whole lot better than anything the Irish had ever known back home. In fact, Irish emigrants writing home to urge their relatives and friends to make the break and come out and share the blessings that the New World had to offer, got into the habit of playing down the American standard of living because they knew that nobody back in Ireland would believe that ordinary people could ever live in such luxury. Michel Chevalier, a French traveller, tells of an Irishman, recently arrived in the United States, who showed his boss a letter he had just written home to his family. 'But, Patrick,' his master asked, 'why do you tell them you have meat three times a week, when you have it three times a day?' And Pat answered: 'Because they wouldn't believe me, if I told them so.'

As well as a reputation for living in filthy, disease-ridden ghettoes, the Irish soon acquired a reputation for spectacular drunkenness. One reason for this may have been the loneliness that many of them felt, so far away from their homes and families, in a land of strange people and unfamiliar customs; but another, undoubtedly, was economic. The Irish labourer could simply never have afforded to get drunk at home; in the States, not only were wages a great deal higher but drink was also an awful lot cheaper.

In his book about the Irish in America, *To the Golden Door* (Boston: Little, Brown, 1960), George Potter gives an illustration of this differential. The price of a gallon of whiskey at Clonmel distillery was 6s. 8d. (less than forty pence in today's money) at a time when, as he put it, 'a shilling [five pence] a day was a better wage than many a good man could obtain, scarcely enough, at that rate, to enable a poor fellow to be drunk for one day with the wages of six. Here, with the means of getting drunk only 29 cents a gallon, and wages a dollar a day, a man could be drunk for a month with the wages of a single day.'

The Irish in America were the first race of 'foreigners' to be forced to accept the abuse and discrimination later to be ladled out to subsequent waves of new immigrants. (I put the word foreigners in quotes because, with the exception of the Red Indians or Amerindians, or native Americans or whatever it is now politically correct to call them, all the American settlers were foreigners.) The sign

'No Irish Need Apply' was used both in relation to jobs and to accommodation. Indeed, all the things that are said today about the Puerto Ricans and the Mexicans and the Cubans were being said a century and a half ago about the Irish. They even enjoyed the distinction of having a political party, the Know-Nothings (so-called because its members were sworn to insist, if questioned, that they knew nothing about anything that had happened) created to harass and, if possible, exterminate them.

But they survived, and gradually managed to climb the social and economic ladder and gain grudging acceptance.

They went into the police force. As the Irish were involved in so many of the saloon brawls and street fights which called for the attention of the cops, even if they weren't always the cause of them, it made good sense to recruit the toughest of them into the force to help curb the belligerence of their compatriots.

They went into the army. Initially the New York Irish military companies were formed, after the failure of the Young Ireland rebellion of 1848, with the idea of sending an expeditionary force back to Ireland to fight for the cause of freedom. Companies with names like the Wolfe Tone Guards, the Napper Tandy Light Artillery and the Irish Patriot Fusiliers may have been recruited to fight on Irish soil for the Irish cause, but their members eventually drifted into the New York State Militia. By 1853, 2,600 of the 6,000 uniformed militia men in the New York area were Irish.

And when, towards the end of the nineteenth century, the railroads were pushed still further west, the Irish again signed on, but now as foremen and bosses. By this time, they had also gravitated into law and politics, fields in which their unrivalled talent for argumentation and disputation proved invaluable.

They founded parish schools in which to educate their children, and later went on to establish institutions of higher learning such as Notre Dame, Fordham, Holy Cross and St Louis. Having themselves noted at first hand the adverse effects of illiteracy, they were determined that their children would get a good education. They identified the Catholic Church in America, formerly French-orientated, as English-speaking, and imposed on it the narrow, puritanical Jansenist attitude that had come to characterise Irish Catholicism.

The Irish in America – even in South America – had their own newspapers, their own charities. Their sons became teachers and doctors, priests and journalists, jobs which by their very nature gave them a power and influence out of all proportion to their numbers, which were in any event very considerable. A September 1994 BBC estimate put the number of Americans claiming some sort of Irish ancestry at forty million, including the so-called Scotch Irish from Ulster.

But it is only fair and realistic to add that the progress made by the Irish in America was not all the unaided work of the Irish emigrants themselves. From the moment that those first wretched, starving Irish emigrants arrived in the United States, the politicians realised that, destitute as they may have been, they all possessed one invaluable piece of capital: a vote apiece. The Irish were understandably flattered when politicians without a drop of Irish blood in their veins took to the Wearing of the Green on St Patrick's Day, and it wasn't long until the habit of persistently wooing the Irish vote became a feature of American politics. And it could be made to work both ways; by utilising the Irish vote to secure themselves a place on the party platforms, the politicians often discovered that they had, in the process, pulled a couple of the Irish up on to the rostrum along with them. It didn't take long, either, for the Irish to discover that if their vote was so valuable to the politicians, they could always put a price tag on it.

'It took 115 years and 6,000 miles and three generations to make this trip, but I'm proud to be here,' said President John F. Kennedy in June 1963, as he stood on the quayside at New Ross, County Wexford, from which his great-grandfather had set sail for America in 1848. Then, pointing to a new fertiliser factory across the River Slaney, he added: 'And if my great-grandfather had not left [Ireland], I might be working over there in the Albatross company.'

Kennedy never forgot his Irish roots, and his four-day visit to the Republic in 1963 probably did more than any other single factor to boost Irish morale and destroy the last vestige of national self-consciousness. In a series of speeches which struck exactly the right tone, Kennedy – eight of whose great-grandparents, he said, had left Ireland in the space of a few months to travel to America – emphasised again and again the deep ties that bound Ireland and the United States together. He took tea and salmon sandwiches with his relatives in front of the family farm at Dunganstown, County Wexford. He sang his favourite Irish rebel song, *Kelly, the Boy from Killane* in a Gaelic football field in New Ross with a crowd of Wexford schoolchildren; and in Dublin he laid a wreath of remembrance on the graves of the executed leaders of Easter, 1916.

And during his Irish visit, he touched on a matter about

which he always felt very strongly: Ireland's unique position as what he called 'a maker and shaper of peace'. He believed that Ireland's influence on the United Nations was far greater than it was reckoned to be, considering its size and position of power in the world of international politics. And he was proved right, because once the Republic of Ireland was accepted as a member of the General Assembly of the United Nations, Ireland began to contribute an influence far out of proportion with its size and importance to that organisation. As one of the generals who was running Ghana in the 1970s when I was there put it, 'The Irish were among the first of the British colonial subject nations to cast off forever the imperial yoke.' As a result, the Irish have always been accepted by the Africans (indeed, at one period, they were known in United Nations circles as the White Africans) in a way that no nation with a colonial past would ever be accepted, and have contributed administrators and adjudicators, as well as peace-keeping troops and aid organisations to distressed countries all over the world. Not to mention the part played by F. H. Boland, a former diplomat and ambassador for Ireland at the Court of St James, who became Secretary-General of the United Nations at what was probably the most crucial period of its existence: the time of the confrontation between Krushchev of the USSR and the whole of the Western world, at a period when the cast of leading players on the world stage included such diverse and intrinsically difficult characters as Eisenhower, Nehru, Macmillan, Tito, Nasser, Sukarno, Nkrumah and Fidel Castro.

On the other hand, the Irish have always resolutely refused to join the North Atlantic Treaty Organisation (NATO), on the grounds that membership would be incompatible with the fact that Irish territory remains partitioned by force by one of the original NATO members, the United Kingdom. Not even membership of what used to be called the EEC and is now known as the European Union, at the same time and on the same basis as Britain, has changed their stance one whit.

Until the 1960s, the Irish who emigrated to England worked mainly as labourers on the railways, the roads and the building sites, or as barmen and barmaids, waiters and waitresses. Many of them still do, but it is surprising how many Irish accents you hear on British television these days among those invited to act as spokesmen for the big multinationals, and it often seems, from their accents, that half the spokesmen for the European Union are Irish too.

In London, not only the barman, but also the postman, the ticket inspector, the doctor who lives around the corner and the man who digs the hole in the road outside your house to repair the water main are likely to turn out to be Irish. So many Irish people are living and working in London that it must rank after Dublin and Belfast, in terms of population, as the third Irish city in the British Isles. Out of the million-odd emigrants born in Ireland now living in England, and not counting the millions of second- and third-generation Irish, it has been estimated that between 300,000 and 400,000 live in London.

It seems that the Irishman emigrated either because he had failed to make the grade at home; and until fairly recently – when Thatcher's obsession with market forces combined with the development of computers and other machines which can do most things far more rapidly and more accurately than people – there were more jobs in

Britain; or he emigrated because he had made the grade and the opportunities for advancement were far greater in a bigger country with a larger population and in general a far higher standard of living.

There is one respect, however, in which the Irish emigrants to Britain differed from the early waves of emigrants who went to America: emigration to Britain could always be regarded, initially, as a temporary expedient. Irishmen went to England because things were slack at home, or because they thought it might enlarge their experience, either of the job or of life itself, or simply because they wanted to get away for a while from parental and family ties. Young women emigrated to sample a taste of a sort of freedom they could rarely find at home, at least until the day before yesterday. In Ireland there's a phrase, normally used to describe people from the country who have done well in the towns and cities: 'They're not long up, but they're well up.' That phrase could now be used for the Irish themselves, and in particular for the Irish women, who now enjoy a freedom that would have been unthinkable even a generation ago.

Emigration to the United States was almost always the result of a firm decision, taken after a great deal of thought; and because it was so expensive to return home again, most of the people who went there had made up their minds to settle there for good. Emigration to Britain, on the other hand, was often the result of a snap decision. A week's wages would pay the fare over, and if things didn't pan out on the other side of the water, another week's wages would pay the fare back home again.

Once in Britain, however, the Irish emigrants soon found that they were developing ties which made it very difficult for them to return. They found, until very recently at any rate, that they could earn far more money than they could ever have hoped to earn in a similar job in Ireland; and they made friends, drifted into marriage and had children. When the children were small, travelling presented problems, and to move back home would have caused a major upset.

Then, as the children got older, they themselves became so integrated both in their lives at school and in the neighbourhood in which they lived, that it seemed unfair to uproot them. And by the time they had grown up, and had started to make their own lives in Britain, it was too late to think about returning to Ireland. In any case, by this time the emigrants would want to remain on in England so that they could visit their own children fairly regularly and watch their grandchildren grow up.

The business of returning to Ireland for holidays also seemed to follow a fairly consistent pattern. (I am using the past tense throughout here, because so many factors in the equation have been altered by the profound and far-reaching changes in life both in Britain and Ireland in the very recent past.) Until the 1970s and 1980s, emigrants to Britain used to return to Ireland fairly frequently, whether they were single, or married with young families. After three or four years, however, they tended to buy caravans, like their neighbours, or take package tours to the Lido de Jessolo or the Costa Brava because that was what their friends and the parents of their children's school friends always did for their holidays.

It was only the extremely well-heeled Irish emigrants – the successful computer-programmers and doctors and nut-crackers, as the Irish call the psychiatrists – who faithfully returned to Ireland, year after year, winter and summer, and who consolidated the Irish tourist victory. What the Irish call a 'soft day' does not in any real way spoil your enjoyment if you are salmon fishing, or shooting, or riding to hounds, but it can make a right hash of a humble family picnic. Also, to the wealthy, Irish hotel prices are a shade less daunting than they are to the middle income groups.

Another point worth making is that the nostalgia which some Irish claim to feel for their native land may well be a simple longing for the open countryside as much as for Ireland itself. Basically, everyone in Ireland comes from a rural background; even Dublin City, with the sea at its feet and the mountains behind it, is 'the country' when compared with cities like Sheffield, Birmingham, Manchester and London, and in many ways feels far more like a holiday resort than a capital city.

Many emigrants long for a sight of the open sea, or a glimpse of the far-off hills – amenities difficult to come by in Britain without travelling huge distances on over-crowded roads – and they confuse this feeling with their love for the old country. Later, when they have sampled the luscious landscapes of Tuscany and Provence, they are often prepared to admit that they would settle for a periodic escape to any less crowded scene. Other Irish emigrants take very kindly to the anonymity of big cities and would not think of exchanging it for any valley of squinting windows, however picturesque.

Also, many Irish emigrants quickly discovered not only the advantages of living in an anonymous society, but also the huge advantage they possessed of being Irish in a highly class-conscious society, like that in Britain. If you are Irish, they cannot easily place you, either by your accent or by your school, in any convenient niche. The class barriers simply do not apply to the Irish at either limits of the social scale, because the Irish, north or south of the border alike, cannot be placed in any social class either by their accent or by the school they attended.

In the late 1960s I wrote a series of articles for the *Irish Times* about the new Anglo-Irish, the Irish emigrants living in Britain, and I discovered in researching these articles that the thousand-dollar question was this: if you had the choice of going back to Ireland now, and were forced to stay there for the rest of your life, or, if you decided against that, you would have to accept that you would never be permitted to visit Ireland again, which would you choose? And I found that the majority of people I interviewed would have elected to stay on in Britain, for any one of a wide variety of reasons.

The real reason they would decide to stay on in Britain, of course, is the one mentioned in Chapter Two: the fact that if they went back to Ireland, they would be regarded as returned empties, with all the magic gone out of them.

But there's a practical side to it, too. A civil servant I talked to said: 'Whatever about living, London is a far better place to work.' A housewife said: 'I try to shake off the feeling of guilt I have about it by telling myself that if my own children never sampled the sheer joy of growing up in a place like Ireland, they wouldn't miss it. Anyway, if we had stayed on in Ireland, the chances are that the children would have emigrated to England themselves in any case. This way, at least, since we're already over here, we can keep in touch with them.'

And Nigel Ryan, from Thurles in County Tipperary, who succeeded Sir Geoffrey Cox, an Australian, in the 1960s as managing director of Independent Television News (ITN), the commercial equivalent of the BBC

News Service, said: 'A disadvantage being Irish in England? Not a bit of it. It's certainly a tremendous disadvantage being Irish over there. But over here, it's a great help.'

And I have to add that although we now spend nearly half of the year in our son's house at Combals, in the Languedoc, in the south of France, and love it there, and visit Ireland as often as we can manage it, I still feel, quite unreasonably, as we approach the cliffs of Dover again on board the car ferry, or the wheels of the plane touch down on the tarmac at Heathrow Airport, that I am coming home.

And like George Moore, I now feel a stranger in Ireland. A returned empty.

15

The Other Six Counties

A Problem of Identity

For those of Saint Patrick's people who stayed on in the old country after the Troubles, there still remained one very tangible remnant of the Irish Question: the border.

It is hard to find any general consensus of opinion on any aspect of the border which separates Saint Patrick's people in the Republic of Ireland from his other people who happen to find themselves living in the area of the island still under British management. This area is variously known as Northern Ireland (though it doesn't include the most northerly county of them all, Donegal); Ulster (though it contains only six of the nine counties of the province of Ulster); and, for obvious reasons, the Six Counties.

There is no general agreement even as to the precise length of this border. I have seen, in official government publications issued on both sides of the border, estimates varying between 280 miles (448 kilometres) and 303 miles (485 kilometres), which is not surprising in view of the casual manner in which it twists and turns its way along the old, eighteenth-century boundaries, bisecting parishes, pubs and premises of all sorts, right down to private houses, in such a way (in villages like Pettigo, County Tyrone, for example, which straddles the border between County Donegal and County Derry) that a man may sleep, as someone put it, with his head under the jurisdiction of the British Crown and his heart in the Irish Republic.

There is no Berlin-type wall marking the border; indeed, until the (fairly) recent Troubles, which started twenty-five years ago and resulted in the arrival of the British Army as the principal peace-keepers in the area, there were only a few manned customs posts at so-called 'approved' border crossings. Before that, the locals used to cross the border several times a day, taking 'unapproved' B-roads and the numberless by-roads and back lanes that straggle the area.

During the worst period of the Troubles all unofficial routes were blocked off, but a man with some local knowledge of the topography, plus a few head of cattle or a flock of sheep to smuggle in and out of the Republic (or Northern Ireland, for that matter) so that they could be counted twice for the purposes of the generous CAP subsidies available from the European Community, could easily find his way across the border through the woods or over the hills. In October 1994, following the IRA cease-fire, the British Prime Minister John Major announced that the road blocks on the border would be removed. But whether the border posts are manned by British soldiers, or merely by customs men, or not at all, the plain truth, whatever the Unionist Ulstermen may like to claim, is that there is no difference whatever in the

Irish landscape immediately north and south of the border, and precious little difference in the people.

I have already made the point that in Celtic, pre-Christian times, and indeed right up until the Elizabethan era, Ulster was the most fiercely Irish and Celtic part of the island. Cuchulain's fortress at Emain Macha was situated more or less on the site of today's Armagh, and it was Armagh which Saint Patrick himself chose as the headquarters of the Christian Church in Ireland; it remains the primacy diocese of both the Protestant and Catholic versions of that faith to this day. Not only that, but Saint Patrick spent the formative years of his early youth herding sheep on the slopes of the Slemish Mountains in County Antrim, and although he chose the mountain called after him (Croagh Patrick near Westport, in County Mayo) as a suitable site for his own retreat into the wilderness, the main place of pilgrimage associated with him, Saint Patrick's Purgatory, is an island in Lough Derg, right on the border between County Donegal and County Tyrone. So it is quite clear that the Six Counties of Northern Ireland were very dear to Saint Patrick's heart, and no wonder, because it's a beautiful part of Ireland.

As I mentioned in the introduction, over the centuries, men have wondered to what extent the character of a race of people is influenced or even determined by the nature of the landscape they happen to inhabit. Is the dark melancholy which seems to afflict so many Russians a reflection of their so often sombre surroundings? And is the casual, carefree attitude of the average Italian due in some measure to the general felicity of the Italian landscape? The question is relevant in relation to the people of Northern Ireland. During the course of nearly four hundred years, many of the descendants of the Lowland Scots and English yeomen who settled in the Six Counties after the Flight of the Earls inter-married and mixed and mingled in less formal contexts with many of the Irish Celts who stayed on in the area after the Plantation, and so, willy-nilly, acquired some of Cuchulain's genes and those of his formidable contemporaries and companions. But by no means did this apply to all of them. Some of the Ulster Lowland Scots and English Protestants preserved their separate identity as zealously as the Boers in South Africa avoided all contact with what they used to call '*thee blicks*' until the recent Mandela revolution. Yet even the most fervent Protestant Ulsterman able to trace an absolutely unbroken, loyalist Protestant lineage back to Robert the Bruce is at heart basically an Irishman, as he very quickly discovers the moment he first sets foot on English soil.

The English draw no distinction whatever between loyal Protestant Ulstermen and rebel Catholic Irishmen from the other three provinces of Ireland: we are all Paddies in their eyes. And they are not in the slightest bit concerned with anybody's religion, a matter which they regard as utterly irrelevant. Cathal Og O'Shannon, the Irish television presenter who recently returned from a trip to Australia, tells me that exactly the same thing applies there, and in New Zealand.

And once they go to live and work in England (or Australia, or New Zealand), the Ulster Protestants instantly realise this, soon begin to accept it and before long start to profit from it, in the same way as what might loosely be called the southern Irish profit from being Irish in England. Indeed, in the course of my own working life, I have met many former Orangemen, who once walked with the very best of them every Glorious Twelfth of July, wearing the sashes their fathers wore, and throwing pennies into the gutter to signify their utter contempt for the Catholic Irish paupers that surrounded them, but who, once they had finally crossed the water, were extremely happy to enjoy all the very considerable advantages of their new status as Irishmen in England.

And even those Ulstermen who never leave the province and who, if queried about their nationality, would unhesitatingly claim to be 'British, through and through' are never for a moment considered by visitors to the area as anything other than Irish. It's a different accent, certainly, but it's unmistakably an Irish accent and not a British or a Scottish one. And, apart altogether from the accent, the Ulstermen all talk like Irishmen, and what is more, drink like Irishmen. It is widely accepted all over Ireland that the 'crack', as they call it in the North, in any bar in Belfast, is every bit as lively and entertaining as the conversation in the average Dublin pub and that the Ulsterman is just as fond of his 'wee jar' as anyone from south of the border.

Nor, as I mentioned in Chapter Eleven, is it without significance that although Union Jacks fly from all the public and indeed many of the private buildings in Northern Ireland, nevertheless in the pubs the measure used for dispensing whiskey is always the generous Irish ball of malt and not the miserable damp patch at the bottom of the glass which constitutes what is laughingly known as a 'large' whiskey in England.

So perhaps the plain truth is that nearly four centuries of exposure to the magical spell still woven by the Irish landscape has turned some at least of those dour, stern Scottish Presbyterians and joyless English Calvinists into

Irishmen in their deepest hearts. If only they would realise it themselves, and admit it, and start rejoicing in the discovery before it's too late, they would make life a lot easier for all the rest of us.

There are, of course, some respects in which Northern Ireland is genuinely different from the Republic. Belfast is the only truly industrialised city on the island of Ireland; Dublin, at the turn of the nineteenth century, had the worst slums in Europe, but they were not industrial slums, and the people were not urban peasants. Unlike Belfast – with its ship-building yards, which launched the *Titanic* ('Even the Pope himself couldn't sink this one,' a Protestant worker at Harland and Wolff remarked as the great ship slid down the slipway into the River Lagan); its aircraft industry, which produced the Short Sunderland, one of the classic planes of the Second World War; and the mills that used to turn out the finest fabric in the world, pure Belfast linen, manufactured from flax grown in Ulster – Dublin never had any large-scale industry, apart from the brewery that manufactures Guinness's stout, and consequently no population of former assembly-line factory workers prepared, in the absence of any prospect of work now or in the forseeable future, to throw stones at one another to help pass the time. In this respect, Belfast is far closer to many cities in what the Unionists insist on calling mainland Britain, places like Leeds or Glasgow, than any Irish city, not that there are any real cities in the Republic outside of Dublin. Cork, the second city, with 80,000 inhabitants, is only about the size of Slough in Buckinghamshire, which is really no more than an Outer London suburb, and Limerick, with 50,000 people, is no bigger than Richmond, Surrey, effectively another Greater London suburb.

But when Home Rule for Ireland began to look like a real possibility in 1912, and the Protestant Unionists of Ulster threatened to take up arms against Britain and go to war with the British, if necessary, in order to remain an integral part of the United Kingdom, Westminster began to consider the possibility of partitioning the island. It is a solution the great powers have often resorted to, for want of a better notion, in Cyprus, in India, in Palestine, in Korea, in Vietnam, and usually with disastrous results.

In Ireland, when the original, pioneering Irish Republican Army had managed to fight the forces of law and order to a standstill in 1921, and had created a situation in which Lloyd George found himself obliged to invite de Valera to London to discuss terms for a peace treaty with him, an all-Ireland independent republic was what most of them were demanding and expecting. But the Unionists managed to pressure the British Prime Minister into partitioning off, not the whole province of Ulster – an area which would have contained far too many Catholic Nationalists to be comfortably contained by the million or so Protestant, pro-British loyalists – nor even the three predominantly Protestant and Unionist counties of Antrim, Armagh and Down – because that area would have been too small to prove viable as an independent unit – but a totally artificial enclave embracing also Derry, Tyrone and Fermanagh, all of them predominantly Catholic and Nationalist.

So when the combined smoke and dust of the War of Independence and the Civil War finally settled down, Saint Patrick's people found themselves sundered by a border leaving three of Ulster's ancient counties, Donegal, Cavan and Monaghan, still in the Free State, and the other six in a Northern Ireland statelet containing the highly explosive mix of one million or so Protestant Unionists, prepared to fight to the death to preserve the Union with Britain, and about half a million Catholic Nationalists who believed that the War of Independence had been all about a free and united Ireland and were not a bit happy about being governed by a Protestant parliament sitting at Stormont. They were, needless to say, immediately subjected to a series of pogroms and turned out of their homes in their thousands by Protestant Unionists who feared – wrongly, as it turned out – that given the Catholic Irish propensity for propagation, they would soon find themselves hopelessly outnumbered.

But it would be a mistake to assume that all the Catholic Nationalists in Northern Ireland were opposed to the maintenance of the Union. Because, at least until relatively recently, the benefits available under the British Welfare State system were far more generous than those on offer in the Republic (the reverse is now the case). Many of the Protestant workers of Northern Ireland also consistently voted for the Conservative (and Unionist) Party; James Connolly, co-founder with James Larkin of the Irish Labour Party, organised the Irish Transport and General Workers Union in and from Belfast, but the Labour Party did not survive in Northern Ireland as a political force with which to be reckoned for very long after Connolly's execution following the 1916 Rising.

In the early days of Stormont's existence as the Parliament of the devolved statelet, there was no opposition. The Protestant workers (as well as many of the Catholic ones) were voting only for the maintenance of the Union and the few Nationalists who succeeded in bucking the system and getting themselves elected to

Stormont refused to recognise the border or even acknowledge Stormont's existence and abstained, as the Sinn Fein Members of Parliament had abstained from attending Parliament in 1919.

To other members of the European Union – and indeed, to most people all over the world today, with the possible exception of most Moslem countries – the Protestant-Catholic divide in Northern Ireland seems utterly baffling. Can anyone understand why, in this day and age, people should be prepared to go to war with one another about a matter which impinges so slightly upon everybody's way of life as religion, of all things?

The answer, of course, is that the Troubles in Northern Ireland are not really about religion at all, and never were. They used to be about privilege, power and position; more recently, they have mostly been about jobs and houses. In the days of the Ulster Plantations, the (Protestant) Scots and English who settled in Ireland on land confiscated from the rebel Irish were allowed to take their choice of the best land available and the most select, usually the most central, parts of the towns, while their (Catholic) Irish neighbours were relegated to the outskirts of the towns, and were allowed to hold on to only the worst land. The pattern of dominance and privilege thus established was maintained over the years, for the very good reason that until the time of Daniel O'Connell, Catholics were not allowed to attend Parliament and so had nobody to stand up for their rights. After they had forced Lloyd George to partition Ireland, along the lines dictated by them, the million or so privileged people, who happened also to be Protestant, were determined to maintain and if possible reinforce that position of privilege in a community which also included roughly half a million less privileged people, who happened also to be Catholic.

This they achieved by gerrymandering the constituencies so that even in areas where they were predominant, Catholics were virtually unrepresented in Parliament – when they eventually decided to attend it and form an opposition – and were grossly under-represented on the local councils.

On the basis that only those people who were actually paying the piper had any right to call the tune, local government was dominated until fairly recently by the privileged Protestants who had made it a rule that only people of property – householders and their wives, and business proprietors, who also enjoyed a company vote on top of their ordinary vote and the like – were entitled to vote in local elections. This naturally resulted in a situation in which the very few jobs and houses that were available went to those who supported the majority on the councils, and they, invariably and inevitably, turned out to be Protestants.

It was as a result of civil rights protests against this situation that the present round of the Troubles in Northern Ireland erupted in 1969. But although the religious divide was used to identify the protagonists, the row wasn't really about religion at all, it was about money. I have always held that if every house in Northern Ireland had two brand-new cars in the garage and a motor-cruiser on a trailer in the driveway, nobody would either know or give a damn about which church, if any, his next-door neighbour happened to attend. But so long as jobs and houses and ready cash remain scarce, Protestant and Catholic are handy labels to differentiate between the haves from the have-nots, and to rally the paramilitaries on both sides.

It must be admitted that over the years since partition there have always been men prepared to kill or be killed, or starve themselves to death for the sake of a united Ireland, as well as men like the Reverend Ian Paisley, who would never entertain the idea of any solution to the problem if it involved any direct dealings with Roman Catholic Dublin. But happily they are in a minority. I am convinced that most of the freedom fighters on both sides were frustrated young men, unable to lay their hands on a job, or any cash with which to acquire a girl, or a car, or even a few drinks to blur the bleakness of their lot, and prepared, in the absence of such amenities, to go along with any activity that promised to make life a bit more exciting than queuing up for the dole or sitting on the sofa watching television. That such people were ruthlessly exploited by more sinister elements on both sides of the border goes without saying. And there has always been an element of tit-for-tat in the Northern Ireland Troubles.

But unless it is all solved by the total political apathy which invariably and inevitably descends on all freedom fighters with the imminent approach of peace and prosperity, the problem – despite the current talks now being hailed as a quantum leap in Anglo-Irish relations – will, in my view, never be solved by democratic discussions around a table because there is no logical solution, and never can be, to any problem in which partition has been desperately grasped as the only possible one. Irish Nationalists, north and south of the border alike, can go on arguing until the cows come home that the basic unit is the whole island of Ireland, inhabited by the final wave of Irish Celts for at least 2,200 years, and defined by and surrounded by the sea. And they can further claim that since, within that unit, an overwhelming proportion of the total population is now and for almost a century has been in favour of an all-Ireland Republic, that is what the island should be. And of course they are right.

But the Northern Ireland Unionists are equally right when they claim that if you take the British Isles as the basic unit, inhabited as it is (including the island of Ireland itself) by a mixed bag of Irish, Welsh and Scots Celts, Picts, Anglo-Saxons, Danes, Normans and increasingly these days by people from all over what used to be the British Empire, not to mention (on the mainland only) a great many descendants of Roman citizens, then it is perfectly logical for a people who find themselves in a majority in one small area of that unit (and they would argue that the border between the Republic and Northern Ireland is neither more nor less logical than that between Belgium and Holland) to vote to abstain from becoming any more closely integrated with a Catholic Irish Republic ruled, as they see it, from Rome. And recent events can only have confirmed the Northern Ireland Protestants in their conviction that Ireland, if not ruled from Maynooth, is certainly run on extremely partisan lines. It is very doubtful whether the Northern Ireland Protestants are any more in favour of abortion than the Catholics in the Republic, but that's not the point. They feel, and rightly, that such matters are for the individual conscience to decide, and not for the hierarchy, nor any government official up to and including the Prime Minister, to interpret what he believes the hierarchy might wish.

So, despite all the high hopes that have been invested in the Reynolds/Major Downing Street Declaration of Christmas 1993, it had always seemed likely that at some stage the Ulster Unionists would realise that they were being asked to surrender far more than they had ever really been prepared to do. And it remained equally possible that at some stage the Irish Republican Army – or some breakaway fragment of it – would question the wisdom of handing over all or even any of its arms to the enemy without having achieved what it has been fighting for, for over seventy years: a united Ireland, totally free of any interference from Britain.

At the end of September 1995, the IRA announced that it was not prepared to make even a token surrender of arms or ammunition as a pre-condition to any effort to revive the flagging peace talks. As most Irish people had been very well aware all along, the IRA would only consider handing its weapons over as part of a general, overall withdrawal of arms in the area, which would also have to include the disarming of the Royal Ulster Constabulary and the withdrawal of British troops from Northern Ireland.

So how does it look as I write this, in October 1995? If the British Government, the European Union and the United States between them can manage to pour enough money into the Northern Ireland economy, it is just possible that the people there may be dazzled into a measure of docility by the glister of gold.

And if the people of the Republic can somehow succeed in persuading the inhabitants of Northern Ireland that they really are Irish under the skin, despite their own misgivings on that subject, and convince them that they might as well profit from being Irish, as they themselves have done, in the context of the European Community, without any grave danger of undue interference from Rome, it is even possible – though not very likely – that they might see that a united Ireland could make economic sense.

But unless, between them, the British and Irish Governments can also create a security situation in which it will be impossible for the IRA, or any fragmented part of it, to operate with impunity ever again, then there is no hope of solving what is left of the Irish Question. For whatever may be agreed around any conference table, it needs only one single nut – or maybe not one, but a few – with a couple of kilos of Semtex to start the whole ghastly business all over again.

There is, of course, always the possibility that the British will find some formula to enable them to pull out of Northern Ireland, leaving their loyal supporters there to carry the can. They have done it so often elsewhere, as the Ulster Unionists are only too well aware, which is one of the factors that makes them so implacable and recalcitrant.

On the other hand, on the very day after Sinn Fein formally announced the IRA decision not to hand over any arms as a precondition to an effort to jump-start the stalled talks again, the new head of the Unionist Party, David Trimble – who succeeded James Molyneux in that position in the late summer – went down to Dublin for talks with the Irish Taoiseach, John Bruton, and sounded faintly optimistic about their outcome. He was the first leader of the Unionist Party to venture south of the border since Terence O'Neill, thirty years earlier, and the only other Unionist leader ever to set foot in what is now the Republic since the foundation of the state of Northern Ireland. It is impossible not to regard this as a hopeful sign. And impossible not to rejoice in the fact that Sinn Fein emphasised that while the IRA were not prepared to surrender any arms as a pre-condition to a resumption of the talks, they were at least prepared to go on talking instead of resuming the shooting.

And the very fact that the whole province of Ulster has enjoyed over fourteen months of fairly normal, peaceful life, with hardly a single shot fired in anger, after a quarter of a century of hell, is going to make everybody think twice about letting anybody reach out for the Semtex again. Or, at least, if some hotheads start itching to pick up their guns again, they may find themselves actively discouraged by their elders and betters and no longer sure of the support of even a small section of the Catholic Nationalist community, a kind of support without which their variety of guerrilla warfare would be impossible.

It would be unrealistic to think that it's over yet, or even that the end is in sight, but perhaps the beginning of the end is now in sight as both sides start to realise, at long last, that they cannot forever go on insisting on their full pound of flesh but must accept some small measure of compromise.

'And will Ireland then be free?' asked the Sean Bhean Bocht, the old lady who personified Ireland at the time of the 1798 Rising, after the arrival of a French invasion force at Killala, in Connemara. Not entirely, would have been the answer, even if the rebellion had been successful.

'Was it needless death after all?' asked W.B. Yeats in his poem 'Easter, 1916'. Again, the answer is probably not really. It is very doubtful if what the Irish achieved in the years following 1916 could have been achieved in any other way.

'And will all that great past,' he asked in another poem, 'be seen as a trouble of fools at the last?' Yet again, the answer can only be, not really. With all the problems that still remain to be solved, Saint Patrick's people have, after all those centuries, re-established their separate identity once and for all, and demonstrated their right to be taken seriously as a nation which is now in a position to offer its compatriots north of the border an independence which they certainly don't have under the existing arrangements imposed by Westminster, and a share in the state where the benefits are basically more generous than in the UK – where the life-style on the whole is of a far higher calibre and, above all, where 'the craic' in general, as the southern Irish call it, is much nearer to 'the crack' in Belfast pubs than the bland waffle you are liable to hear in English pubs.

There is hope, too, in the fact that when the 1995 Nobel Prize for Literature was won by the Ulster poet, Seamus Heaney – the fourth Irish writer to receive the world's most prestigious literary prize in the ninety-three years it has been in existence – his first reaction was to say that he regarded it as a prize not for himself, but for Ireland. And by Ireland, he meant all Ireland.

But perhaps the greatest hope of all lies in a new concept of a federal Ireland, which is gradually gaining support everywhere. Basically, the idea is that the four ancient provinces of Ireland, Ulster (the whole province, not just the Six Counties), Munster, Leinster and Connacht, should each have their own autonomous, elected assemblies, which would reflect their own complex mix of regional cultures, traditions and sociological and economic needs.

Ultimate power would no longer be centralised from Dublin or Belfast, but perhaps shared by an elected president and an elected federal parliament – a natural successor to the Ard Ri or High King of Ireland, who was also always elected by the people – which would be based in a neutral area acceptable to the whole of Ireland, such as Tara, the ancient capital of the Irish High Kings.

A return, in other words, to the way in which Ireland was organised and arranged when Saint Patrick returned to the scene in AD 432 to begin to convert and adopt his people. It could well work.

Appendix

Gaelish: A Note on the Pronunciation of Irish

It is very difficult for anyone educated only or mainly through English to reproduce accurately the correct pronunciation of most words in Irish Gaelic, just as it is extremely difficult, if not almost impossible, for English-speaking people to pronounce the French 'r' or the Spanish 'c' or 'g' correctly. To get over this problem, various simplified mongrel languages, such as the Franglais used by Myles Kington and others, have been invented, and I now offer some hints on approximate pronunciations of some of the Irish Gaelic words used in the text of this book. If you follow my over-simplified, vaguely phonetic renderings of these words correctly, you will not be speaking Irish Gaelic, by any means, but there is a fair chance that the relatively few people in Ireland who do speak some Irish Gaelic will know what you are trying to say. I suppose you could call this version of the Irish language Gaelish.

I put a footnote under the first Irish words I used, Tir

na nOg (Land of Youth) and suggested Tear-nan-Ogue as a possible equivalent in English. There is no true equivalent, because Irish Gaelic has sounds that are unlike any sounds in the English language and accents which are so archaic that they do not even appear, so far as I am aware, in the extended vocabulary of any computer printer. For example, I haven't been able to find any combination of computer keys that will give you a 'b' with a dot over it – known in Irish as a *'b' buailte* (pronounced 'b' boo-all-cha) – which is essential in Irish Gaelic. It is pronounced as a 'v', and was reproduced in the form of Irish Gaelic used by the early governments of the Irish state for documents printed in Roman type as 'bh'. This didn't make a lot of sense to people either educated only in Irish or only in English, and explains why many West Britons, who were confused by the new names the Irish started giving to all the old, familiar places as soon as they regained a measure of independence from their next-door neighbours in the early 1920s, were dismayed when Queenstown, in County Cork, was renamed Cobh (pronounced Cove) and always referred to it as Cob H in their confusion.

Similarly, when the port a few miles to the south of Dublin City which for generations had been known as Kingstown reverted to its ancient name of Dun Laoghaire (the fort of Leary, and pronounced doon-leary), English visitors rarely got any closer to the correct pronunciation than Done Lock Hair.

And during all the years – from 1937 to 1949 – when Ireland was officially known as Eire (the Gaelic word for Ireland, pronounced Air-eh) it was almost invariably pronounced 'Air', even by BBC newscasters, who should have known better.

And 'b' is not the only consonant that comes in the *buailte* form. An *m buailte*, that is to say an 'm' with a dot over it, reproduced in Roman script as 'mh', is pronounced either as a 'v' as in Niamh (Neeve) or as a 'w' as in Comhaltas (pronounced Co-wall-thas). A *t buailte* (in Roman, 'th') is pronounced as an 'h', as in Tuatha de Danaan (Two-ha de Da-nawn). A *d buailte* (in Roman, 'dh') is not pronounced at all, so the the word *sidhe*, meaning fairy, is pronounced shee, and *filidh*, meaning poet, becomes feeley.

Vowels also present considerable problems in Irish Gaelic. The ancient king of Leinster who was primarily responsible for the invasion of Ireland by Henry II's Anglo-Norman barons was offering his beautiful daughter Aoife in return for some military assistance in overcoming the Irish High King. Aoife is pronounced Eef-eh, and in general the vowels 'aoi', when encountered together, are pronounced as 'ee' as in Taoiseach, pronounced Tee-shock, or Naoise, pronounced Nee-sheh. Oisin looks a bit puzzling, but if you meet someone who spells his name that way, it is a fair bet that if you were to address him as Usheen, he would know that you were trying to engage him in conversation. Similarly, anyone called Maebh will answer to Maeve, and anyone called Siobhan will recognise Shivawn as a fair approximation.

Caoilte can, when spoken by a true Gael, have as many as five or six separate and subtle syllables, but Keel-cha, with a soft 'ch' as in 'cha-cha-cha', will be understood. And although it has now become very fashionable to christen your children, giving them names from Celtic mythology, you are unlikely to meet anyone called Cuchulain, which means 'the hound of Cullen'; if you do, however, Koo-hullen is a fair approximation, because a *c buailte* almost, though not entirely, disappears in spoken Irish.

You are also unlikely to need such words as *dibhinn criochnaitheach* (final dividend), but if you are curious to know what it sounds like, dee-veen creek-na-chock is a fairish stab at it. *Fir* (pronounced fear) is the word for men and the word is also used to indicate the proximity of a gents' toilet; *mna* (pronounced m-naw) means women, and is also used for a women's toilet. *Uisghe beatha*, pronounced ish-geh baha, means water of life and is the word from which whiskey was derived.

Acknowledgements

I should like, first of all, to thank John Ardagh for giving me permission to quote from his book, *Ireland and the Irish*; and to the Peters, Fraser and Dunlop Group Ltd for permission to use an extract from Frank O'Connor's translation of Bryan Merriman's *Midnight Court*. Every effort has been made to trace copyright owners of material used in this book; where acknowledgement has been omitted, the author is happy to make the appropriate acknowledgement in future editions.